Concern for Anabaptist Renewal

CONCERN for Anabaptist Renewal

A Radical Reformation Reader, 1971

CONCERN: A Pamphlet Series for
Questions of Christian Renewal

EDITED BY
Laura Schmidt Roberts and Virgil Vogt

WIPF & STOCK · Eugene, Oregon

CONCERN FOR ANABAPTIST RENEWAL
A Radical Reformation Reader, 1971

CONCERN: A Pamphlet Series for Questions of Christian Renewal

Copyright © 2022 Wipf and Stock Publishers. All rights reserved. Except for brief quotations in critical publications or reviews, no part of this book may be reproduced in any manner without prior written permission from the publisher. Write: Permissions, Wipf and Stock Publishers, 199 W. 8th Ave., Suite 3, Eugene, OR 97401.

Wipf & Stock
An Imprint of Wipf and Stock Publishers
199 W. 8th Ave., Suite 3
Eugene, OR 97401

www.wipfandstock.com

PAPERBACK ISBN: 978-1-6667-3656-4
HARDCOVER ISBN: 978-1-6667-9507-3
EBOOK ISBN: 978-1-6667-9508-0

Contents

Editor's Note | vii
Foreword by John Roth | ix
Introduction by Virgil Vogt | 1

1   The Recovery of the Anabaptist Vision | 3
      JOHN HOWARD YODER

2   The Mennonite Conception of the Church and Its Relation to Community Building | 21
      HAROLD S. BENDER

3   The Anabaptist Theology of Discipleship | 32
      HAROLD S. BENDER

4   Anabaptist Studies 1–5 | 40
      WILLIAM KLASSEN

5   Radical Reformation 1–5 | 98
      WALTER KLAASSEN

6   The Pacifism of the Sixteenth-Century Anabaptists | 146
      HAROLD S. BENDER

      Anabaptism: An Introductory Bibliography (unattributed) | 161
      Appendix: Listing of all *Concern* republication volumes | 163

      Bibliography | 171

Editor's Note

This volume completes republication of *Concern: A Pamphlet Series for Questions of Christian Renewal* (1954–1971). An appendix lists the contents of the seven total volumes comprising the *Concern* republishing project initiated under the editorial direction of Virgil Vogt and completed by Laura Schmidt Roberts.[1]

The republication of *Concern* no. 18 comes after significant unanticipated delay. The Foreword by John Roth, written in 2013, reflects a context before fuller evidence of a long-standing pattern of sexual abuse by *Concern* writer and sometime editor, theologian and ethicist John Howard Yoder, became public.[2] This reality problematizes the standing of Yoder's work in ongoing Anabaptist-Mennonite scholarship. While significant deconstruction of Yoder's corpus has been done, grappling with the aftermath and implications of so mixed a legacy continues. Refusing to engage or promote

---

1. In addition to this volume, two previously published volumes edited by Vogt (*The Roots of CONCERN*, 2009; *CONCERN for Education*, 2010) and a 2022 four-volume, thematically organized series edited by Roberts (*CONCERN for the Church in the World*, *CONCERN for Church Renewal*, *CONCERN for Church Mission and Spiritual Gifts*, *CONCERN for Church Polity and Discipline*) complete the Wipf and Stock republication of the *Concern* pamphlets.

2. In 2015 historian Rachel Waltner Goossen published a crucial article revealing the full extent of Yoder's sexual abuse in the *Mennonite Quarterly Review*, a journal edited by Roth. See Waltner Goossen, "'Defanging the Beast.'" In the essay Waltner Goossen catalogs both Yoder's serial sexual abuse and the institutional failure to respond adequately to his victims or Yoder himself. Other articles in that special issue of MQR addressed larger questions related to sexual violence in the church and opened the complicated discussion regarding Yoder's theological legacy that has continued in many other venues. See for example Anabaptist Mennonite Biblical Seminary, "AMBS Response to Victims"; Cramer et al., "Theology and Misconduct"; Soto Albrecht and Stephens, *Liberating the Politics of Jesus*.

Editor's Note

Yoder's work as a whole or selectively is one avenue of response. Another avenue of response takes encounters with his thought (in church, in institutions, in print) as an occasion to reframe discussion of it by first speaking the truth of his sexual abuse. Having done so here, readers are invited to reconsider work by Yoder in this volume in light of that context.

Laura Schmidt Roberts
Fresno Pacific University
September 2021

Foreword

In the middle of the twentieth century, two events occurred that changed the trajectory of Anabaptist-Mennonite scholarship and played a decisive role in shaping the essays that appear in this volume. Harold S. Bender's "The Anabaptist Vision"—first presented as the presidential address to the American Society of Church History in December of 1943 and then published in *Church History* and *The Mennonite Quarterly Review* several months later—marked a symbolic turning point in the general perception of Anabaptism among mainstream church historians and theologians. In sharp contrast to the prevailing assumption that sixteenth-century Anabaptism was a sectarian perversion of Reformation principles, Bender described the early Anabaptists as pioneers of religious liberty—earnest Christians whose commitment to believers baptism, Christian discipleship, and an ethic of love represented the true fulfillment of Reformation Biblicism and pointed the way toward the modern principle of separation of church and state. Over time "The Anabaptist Vision" marked the entry of the Radical Reformation into broader Reformation scholarship and signaled a new era of theological confidence among North American Mennonites who were gradually moving from tightly-knit agrarian communities into the world of higher education, the professions and the suburbs.

Only a few years later, a small group of Bender's students, drawing explicitly on lessons learned from "The Anabaptist Vision," launched a reform movement that was deeply critical of Bender and the Mennonite Church he represented. In the spring of 1952 a group of young Mennonite relief workers, serving in Europe under Mennonite Central Committee, gathered in Amsterdam to share their frustrations regarding the state of the church and their vision for a renewed Mennonite witness that more closely reflected the radical witness of the sixteenth-century Anabaptists. Indeed, in an odd way, the group replicated the experience of the first generation of Anabaptists who had gathered excitedly around Zwingli in the early 1520s, only to be disappointed by his diffidence and caution. Led by John H. Yoder,[3] who was to become the movement's most visible representative, the Amsterdam group soon broadened their circle and gave voice to their criticism in a publication series they called "*Concern*."

The essays gathered in this volume—Number 18 in the *Concern* series—vividly capture the intellectual and theological energy of the day. Each of the contributions by Harold Bender, for example, are elaborations on the three central themes of "The Anabaptist Vision"—the church as a voluntary community of believers; Christian faith expressed as discipleship (Nachfolge Christi); and the centrality of love in all human relations. Bender's essays eloquently defend the distinctive themes of Anabaptist thought and his understanding of their relevance for the contemporary church.

Yoder's contribution, which he titled "The Recovery of the Anabaptist Vision," is explicitly indebted to Bender, and offers a clear apology for the place of Anabaptist studies within the broader history of the Reformation. But a closer reading of Yoder's essay—along with the introduction by Virgil Vogt—reveals the deeper tensions between Bender and his students. Yoder and his colleagues read the same Anabaptist sources as Bender, but they drew more radical conclusions about their consequences, particularly in terms of ecclesiology. Thus in the final section of his essay ("Anabaptism vs. Mennonites") Yoder argued that the "historical meaning of Anabaptism, which is biblically justified, is not identical with but in serious conflict with contemporary Mennonitism." The church must either commit itself fully to the Anabaptist vision, he insisted, or "conclude honestly that out of faithfulness to the Anabaptist vision the Mennonite denomination should cease to exist."[4]

In a slightly less polemical vein, Walter Klaassen and William Klassen drew on the latest scholarship of the day in offering normative Anabaptist perspectives on a host of historical and theological themes. No less than Bender and Yoder, their essays reflect a deep conviction that

---

3. This volume contains work by John Howard Yoder, whose sexual abuse is a well-established fact which must be acknowledged. Please see the Editor's Note for more about the choice to republish Yoder's work.

4. Yoder, "Recovery," essay in this volume, 20.

sixteenth-century Anabaptism can provide an authoritative basis to address the challenges faced by the contemporary church.

That confident assumption that the past could offer clear theological lessons for the present, an assumption shared by all the contributors to the volume, would soon come under fierce attack. In 1972 Claus-Peter Clasen's *Anabaptism: A Social History* and James Stayer's *Anabaptism and the Sword*—followed three years later by a seminal essay, "From Monogenesis to Polygenesis," in *The Mennonite Quarterly Review*—signaled a new era in Anabaptist studies. By the late 1970s, students of the Radical Reformation brought increasing attention to the social, economic, and political context of Anabaptism that complicated earlier assumptions about goals and motivation. The simple narrative of Anabaptist beginnings in Zurich, favored by Bender, fragmented into a host of divergent, sometimes competing, expressions of radical reform. And as Anabaptist studies found a foothold within the larger academy, the very notion of doing "scholarship for the church" became intellectually problematic.

Clearly, much has changed in Radical Reformation scholarship since the publication of *The Radical Reformation Reader*. But in a world increasingly skeptical of the Constantinian assumptions of the past, where doubts about the future of the institutional church are widespread, and a hunger for authentic Christianity deepens, the essays gathered in this volume continue to speak with clarity and vibrancy. They remind us that Jesus continues to call his followers to metanoia—to repentance, to conversion, to a new direction—rooted in daily discipleship, more radical forms of community, and a deep commitment to loving all of God's children, including the poor, the marginalized, and the enemy.

John D. Roth
Goshen, Indiana
Fall, 2013

Introduction

Every scribe who has been trained for the kingdom of heaven is like a householder who brings out of his treasure what is new and what is old.

—MATT 13:52

In this issue of *Concern*, we want to participate in the process described by Jesus, sharing in the creation of a unique Christian witness which is adequate to the needs of our time.

We are bringing out something old. Here is the legacy of a radical Christian movement which took shape more than 400 years ago. In its day it was something new—an exciting and authentic sample of God's kingdom finding fulfillment in human history. Its evangelistic vigor, its stand on voluntary membership by means of adult commitment, its radical discipleship, Christian communalism, shared economics, and profound nonviolence, have all become part of our common history.

There is an aspect of newness, however, even in the retelling of this old story. It is only within the last two generations that the efforts of historical scholarship have given it back to us in a faithful and understandable manner. John Yoder's article sketches the way in which this actually took place. The rediscovery of this story has been a new and exciting event for a good many Christians in our time.

Yet there is something very unfinished about a collection of articles on Christian radicalism which must draw so heavily upon the experiences of another century. The kingdom teacher must also bring out what is new. The message of this collection is like a partially completed painting. The new part remains to be added with the same clarity as that which has gone into what is old.

It is significant that all of the writers have a personal lifestyle which is much less radical than that of the sixteenth-century movements about which they report. For the most part, they have made their contributions within established churches and church institutions. They have taken significant and courageous stands on a variety of specific issues, but they have not been involved in the creation of radically new forms of church life. This may explain why the picture remains unfinished.

What the kingdom of God requires is a radical Christian movement in our own time which has a vigor and depth which equals that of those radicals who have gone before us. We cannot, however, do a rerun of what happened in the sixteenth century. While some issues remain the same, new ones arise. Thus, a combination of what is old and what is new will be the only viable form, as Jesus explained.

Fortunately, the ingredients for this radical Christian movement are much more in evidence now than they were a few years ago. The unfaithfulness of the mainline denominational churches is becoming more and more apparent. The number of persons who are ready to risk all in an attempt to create other alternatives has also grown phenomenally. That such an alternative will require re-creation of the communal aspects of Christianity, that it will require radically new patterns of economic life, total commitment to nonviolence, and a surrender of individualism, are insights which keep cropping up in the most surprising places and with encouraging frequency.

It is undoubtedly these new Christian radicals who must fill out certain missing elements in the creation of a witness adequate for our time. But it will be a better and more profound witness if it can incorporate the lessons of an earlier century.

The articulation and development of the kingdom of God is as cumulative and progressive as the study of natural science. What we publish in this issue of *Concern* are reports from a series of experiments which could be rather valuable to those who are now working on the experimental frontiers of the Christian movement.

Virgil Vogt
May 31, 1971

1

The Recovery of the Anabaptist Vision[1]

John Howard Yoder

I. Scholarly Development in Its Sociological Context

The significance of what has come to be called "the recovery of the Anabaptist vision" can best be understood by seeing it within the social experience of American Mennonitism. Between 1900 and 1930, American Mennonites found themselves entering increasingly into the educational and intellectual world around them. That world was itself in the throes of serious theological conflict, offering to Mennonite young persons as they entered the academic world a ready-made set of alternatives for their loyalty.

On the one hand there was the tradition of theological liberalism, with its far-reaching criticism of traditional Christian insights and its optimistic expectations for the improvement of American civilization. On certain superficial levels, such as interests in philanthropy and peace, there were some features within this tradition to which Mennonites could well be sympathetic, and a few significant early intellectual leaders took this tack; it was symbolized also by the membership of one of the Mennonite

1. Lecture presented to a Student Services Summer Seminar, Elkhart, IN, August 1964.

conference bodies in the Federal Council of Churches during the years of its formation.

For the main body of the Mennonite churches such an alliance was, however, not possible. It was inconsistent not only with the simple biblical faith of the mass of believers, but also with the earlier more exploratory contacts which Mennonite leaders had in the nineteenth century with the spokesmen of evangelical Protestantism, especially through the Sunday school movement and the revivalism of Moody.

It was therefore no surprise that Mennonites found their intellectual and institutional sympathies more on the side of mainline historic Protestantism with its firmly rooted loyalties to the Bible and to Christian history. But mainline Protestantism on its side already had a traditional and official understanding of the Mennonites. Protestantism, especially of the Lutheran and Reformed traditions, but to a large degree also the other younger Protestant bodies, understood the identity of Protestantism as having been established by the polemic position it had taken during the sixteenth century. Protestantism at that time meant a break with the Roman Catholic Church because of that church's emphasis on good works. Protestantism further meant a break with the so-called "fanatic left wing" of the Reformation time, from whom the Lutheran and Reformed leaders turned away for two very good reasons. One of these reasons was that the fanatics gave too much free play to what they called "the spirit," uncritically opening themselves to all sorts of excesses, to claims of special revelation, and otherwise threatening the order of the church. Yet at the same time these same fanatics were accused of being too literalistic, taking certain Bible passages at face value instead of realizing that they needed to be "interpreted" in order to fit the European "state church" situation.

Beyond this initial polemic understanding of the meaning of Protestantism, the Lutheran tradition understood its reasons for rejecting the Reformed, and the Reformed likewise has spent centuries in interpreting its rejection of the Lutheran, each saying in its way that the other group was too Roman and too fanatic. The Lutherans felt that the Reformed were too Catholic because church leaders attempted to give instructions to political leaders, and too fanatic because they did not believe in the miracle of sacramental transformation. For the Reformed, the Lutherans were too Catholic because of their view of the sacraments and too fanatic in their unconcern for the divinely willed social order.

Now for the Mennonites (Anabaptists) to come on the scene was for them to fit into the categories already clearly established by centuries of the partisan reading of history. On every count, their witness was understood either as a sectarian fanaticism or as a renewed kind of works religion.

Not only in the sixteenth century was Mennonite identity under a cloud. Mennonites in the beginning of our century faced a somewhat similar problem in being understood in contemporary terms. It was just during this same period, 1900–1930, that under the leadership of Ernst Troeltsch theology was beginning to speak the language of sociology and to think of minority groups as expressing a peculiar social pattern by the use of religious terms. This could mean that a "sectarian" group could be respected because of its reflecting its own social history (in this case, German, agricultural, and morally optimistic) but by the same token would have nothing to say to churches of other social traditions.

II. The Recovery of Anabaptist History

Since the way in which the other church traditions had identified Mennonitism was the product of their reading of history, it was most appropriate that the first efforts of modern Mennonite scholarship should have centered on the renewed, corrected reading of the Reformation story. The scholarly study of the history of the Anabaptists, as opposed to the polemic reporting of earlier ages, really began about 1860. It was carried further, especially as far as the Zurich reformation was concerned, beginning in the first part of this century by Emil Egli, Walther Köhler, and Fritz Blanke. In the beginning of the period of which we are speaking, the study of history was begun within the Mennonite tradition by the German scholars Hege, Neff, and the immigrant John Horsch, carrying on, as far as North America was concerned, the institutional impetus which had come from the publishing work of John F. Funk and his republication of Anabaptist documents.

This entire process came to a sort of first fruition beginning around 1930 with the scholarly production of C. Henry Smith, Harold S. Bender, Ernst Correll, and Cornelius Krahn. Its major vehicle was *The Mennonite Quarterly Review* and more recently *The Mennonite Encyclopedia*. It might be said that this period was culminated by the attempted summaries and definitions brought together in 1957 by the Guy F. Hershberger volume whose title the present lecture borrows. It is the product of this generation of research and rediscovery which we now seek to report upon.

III. What Happened in the Sixteenth Century?

The earlier traditional Protestant polemic reading of history proceeded by placing in one classification as "fanatic" everything which did not belong in the major state-church categories of Lutheran, Reformed, Anglican, or Roman Catholic Christianity. It was by placing all these dissenters under one heading that the devastating rejection of everything thus classified was enabled. A major portion of the clarification in our generation comes from establishing clear distinctions among the dissenters of the Reformation Age.

A. Andreas Bodenstein von Carlstadt

Carlstadt had been the theological teacher of Martin Luther and was until 1525 his respected colleague. It, however, became increasingly clear that Carlstadt was taking the Bible more literally than Luther and was more concerned for the consistent application of its teachings. He therefore questioned the baptism of infants and rejected the use of "images" in the church. It was also he who for the first time initiated, in the temporary absence of Martin Luther, a more Protestant practice of the Lord's Supper. Luther, feeling that this extreme position of Carlstadt would endanger his entire Reformation, leagued himself with the political authorities to restrain and finally to expel Carlstadt. Although he rejected infant baptism in principle, Carlstadt never practiced believer's baptism, nor did he seek the establishment of a church independent of the state. Although he did establish communication with the "Anabaptists" at Zurich, his loyalty ultimately was attached not to them but to the Reformed tradition of Zurich and Strasbourg.

B. Thomas Müntzer

Müntzer was as well a Lutheran, but a highly inflammatory public preacher convinced (at least later in his activity) that he had special visionary insights into God's purposes. He rejected, or at least challenged, the practice of infant baptism, though without practicing any other form, and castigated the superficiality or unreality of the faith of most people. In 1525 he joined forces with the revolutionary peasants in their hopeless uprising against the German princes.

We know of no contact between Müntzer and those who later came to be called "Anabaptists"; he never practiced baptism on confession of faith, nor did he constitute a free congregation.

C. The Swiss Brethren

It is this movement which has been seen, especially through the studies of Blanke and Bender, to be the real source of what we later will have reason to call "mainstream Anabaptism." The origins of this movement were within the Zurich Reformation, led primarily by a circle of young men who began as earnest disciples of Huldrych Zwingli; who, however, lost confidence in his leadership when it became clear that he was ready to move the Reformation forward no faster than the city council would permit.

Of the intertwined issues which finally led to the formation of an independent movement, the authority of the Bible (as over against that of the political leaders), the existence of a free church formed by voluntary association of committed believers (as over against a state church constituted by infant baptism), the frequent practice of the Lord's Supper, not as a sacrament with special ritual significance but with ordinary bread and wine in homes, and the baptism of committed believers were the major marks. Through a conversational development leading from late 1523 to early 1525, there came about the formation on January 21, 1525, of this first free church movement through the institution of believer's baptism.

Although soon bereft of its major leaders, this movement was able to maintain its identity, expressed most strongly in early 1527 by the drafting of a confessional document, the Schleitheim "Brotherly Understanding."

D. The Radicals of Eastern Switzerland

Independently of the movement at Zurich there was also developing in 1523–25 a dissenting group in Eastern Switzerland, especially St. Gall. Although the idea and the practice of believer's baptism were brought here from Zurich and there was considerable mutual acquaintanceship in 1525, this movement had its own character both before and after its contacts with the Zurich Anabaptists. It was more "separatist" than they in its willingness to cut off conversation with other Christians, it was more "inspirationist" in the conceptions its leaders had of divine guidance, and it was more ready than they to take advantage of the social resentment of the lower classes. Its inspirationism expressed itself in strange ways, including rare (but highly publicized) criminal offenses. Most of its members under the pressure of persecution returned to the state churches. It was probably the liberty taken by some representatives of this trend which led to the Schleitheim meeting with its concentration on responsible church order.

E. Melchior Hofmann

Melchior Hofmann began his churchly career as a disciple of Martin Luther, came then to share the views of Zwingli, and finally in 1530 initiated a movement of his own, beginning in Strasbourg. His position was characterized by very peculiar understandings of the meanings of biblical texts, usually illuminated by a doctrine of symbolic meanings; although not himself a visionary, he was willing to accept as revelation the visions received by others, and he held a deviant view of the incarnation, according to which Jesus did not receive his flesh from his human mother. Although acquainted with the Swiss Brethren, Hofmann acted independently of them in establishing the practice of believer's baptism for his own adherents, and thereby established a separate organizational tradition. It was Hofmann who was responsible for taking the "Anabaptist" idea to the Netherlands in this peculiar form. He was really active only from 1530 to 1533 as an Anabaptist; from then on until his death he was in prison in Strasbourg.

F. Münster

At the time of his imprisonment in Strasbourg, Melchior Hofmann instructed his disciples in the Netherlands to lay low, even abstaining from the practice of baptism, until the Lord would bring about the great events of the end of time. Later, however, some leaders among these disciples received new "revelations" on the basis of which they terminated the waiting period and again took matters into their own hands. They moved to the city of Münster in Northern Germany, which was already in the process of both social and religious upheaval, led at that time by Bernhard Rothmann, a man with convictions much like those of Huldrych Zwingli. Between 1533 and 1535, the city of Münster was utterly transformed in line with the new revelations which these men received on all sorts of subjects, including the institution of polygamy. For them, the Old Testament was placed above the New and the war by which Münster defended itself was a holy crusade. The practice of adult baptism was maintained, as a carryover from the heritage of Melchior Hofmann, but now it was a compulsory act of loyalty to the state church and no longer an expression of voluntary discipleship commitment. The city of Münster fell before the armies of the bishop and the neighboring provinces in 1535.

G. Menno

Going beyond Melchior Hofmann's tradition in another direction we find Menno Simons, who entered their movement in 1536, after the disciples of Hofmann were seriously dismayed, some of them having followed Münster, others having rejected violence but all finding themselves now without leadership. It was largely Menno to whom the credit must go not only for reorganizing the Dutch Anabaptist churches but especially for stating their understanding of the Christian faith in a form which was able to survive. The position to which Menno himself had come was very similar to that of the Swiss Brethren-Schleitheim tradition, although between that tradition and himself there was no direct tie, but rather a chain of relationships with several gaps in it. He did maintain from the legacy of Hofmann his somewhat different understanding of the meaning of the humanity of Jesus, and differed as well from the Swiss Brethren in the severity with which he was willing to apply as a tool of church discipline the "avoidance" of the excommunicated.

H. Free Spirits

Under this heading may be brought together a group of highly stimulating and attractive individual personalities, none of whom, however, carried his criticism of accepted religious patterns to the point of establishing a church fellowship. Some of them were entirely independent teachers or writers; others did gather about them groups of disciples whom they, however, did not want to constitute as Christian brotherhoods. Their critical attitudes toward Catholicism and state-church Protestantism were similar to those of the Swiss Brethren, but they rejected the goal of restoring an organized church life which would seek to be less unfaithful to biblical standards.

I. Denck, Hubmaier, Hut

Under this heading we bring together men whose only common distinguishing trait was that they were strong individuals, acquainted with each other in the early Anabaptist movement, but none of whom established a permanent separate group. Hans Hut differed from the other two and from the other Swiss Brethren in his preoccupation with the coming end of the world; Hans Denck was a more philosophical and speculative person; and

Balthasar Hubmaier did not share the conviction of other Anabaptists concerning the use of violence by the state. In spite of the unique origins and contributions of each of these men, what they produced and left behind became in each case part of the common heritage of the Swiss Brethren-South German movement.

J. The Bruderhof

In 1528 one tiny group of Anabaptist refugees established, under the pressure of persecution, a common congregational purse. This pattern of life was solidified into a permanent institution under the leading of Jacob Hutter, for whose sake the group sometimes carries the name "Hutterian Brethren." Only this unique pattern of economic organization distinguishes the Bruderhof from the Swiss Brethren; in other respects, their convictions are the same and during the sixteenth century they recognized one another as related groups.

K. Pilgram Marbeck

Coming into the Anabaptist movement where it had been planted in Austria by Hans Hut, Marbeck became its main spokesman in Strasbourg around 1530, and for the next generation was the most significant leader and writer of the South German movement. His basic position is the same as that of the Swiss Brethren and Schleitheim; he had occasion to concern himself especially with the need for spiritual unity among the various Anabaptist groups and to delve deeper into the formulating of theological convictions than had the leaders of the earlier years.

L. Antitrinitarians

Catalogues of the dissenters of the sixteenth century are not complete without including reference to the Antitrinitarians. These men had no immediate relationship to Anabaptism during the early days, although contacts were established later in Poland. There might be some similarity between some of their ideas and the speculative thought of Hans Denck.

Now that we have come to recognize that it is not fair historically to assume that all of these movements and figures belong together, so that we can apply indiscriminately to all of them the weaknesses and the heresies of each, how are they to be understood and classified? Four of the figures listed were in no sense Anabaptists: Carlstadt, Müntzer, the Free Spirits, and the early Antitrinitarians raised no questions about the structure of the

Christian community and drew no practical conclusions from their doubts about the baptism of infants.

Some of the other groups may *properly* be referred to as "fanatic" because of the special claims they made to unique divine revelation and their lack of orderliness in putting their critique of society into practice. Thomas Müntzer, the radicals of St. Gall, and Münster were all very brief experiences, the first two leaving no traces beyond 1527 and the third being crushed within two years, less than ten years later.

Of the above groups and figures, only the Antitrinitarians survived beyond 1540. We then have left to consider as "mainstream Anabaptists," the traditions of the Swiss Brethren (C), Menno (G), the strong individual Anabaptists (I), the Bruderhof (J), and Marbeck (K). Scholars are still discussing whether these groups should be classified under three, four, or five subheadings, but for our purposes it should be sufficient to see the enormous breadth of the agreement between them. Should any subdivisions be necessary, it should suffice to think of three: of the Menno tradition as different with its doctrine of the incarnation and the practice of the ban, of the Bruderhof with its economic pattern, and of the "Swiss Brethren." We move then to the study of the position of this "mainstream Anabaptism."

IV. The Church Is Visible

Before the baptism of infants and of believers became a debating issue between Huldrych Zwingli and his young followers, their first clash had to do with whether the Christian community is to take on some sort of form distinct from the larger society and the state. Zwingli had initially believed in the formation of a free and visible community of believers but moved away from the idea when he saw the opposition which it called forth on the part of the city authorities of Zurich. He also was concerned initially for a serious practice of spiritual discipline according to the model of Matt 18:15–18 but relinquished this in favor of a "moral police" responsibility entrusted to city government. In saying that the Christian church need not take upon itself any particular outward form, since any outward form is in any case not perfect or fully faithful, Zwingli took over the argument of the free spirits, not in order to avoid having any church patterns at all, but in order to justify his leaving these matters in the hand of the state.

It is one trait of the "visibility" of the church that it is not possible to distinguish Christian morality from belief. "Discipleship" was a major dimension of the Anabaptist understanding of what faith means; there is no faith and no church without following Christ in one's life. With a view to the structure of the church, this means that the church is a voluntary community. With regard to the logic of ethical thinking, it means that Christian behavior is Christological, drawing its guidance not from a set of general philosophical principles nor a collection of codified precise obligations, but from the person and the teachings of Jesus. This understanding of Christian ethics as following Christ was a source of the nonresistant conviction of the early Anabaptists and their understandings of the state and of martyrdom (at this point see Schleitheim).

It follows also from the visibility of the church that there need to be organs, distinct from those of the state, for the consultation and management of the Christian body. So it was that the Anabaptists came together not only in local congregations but also in broader geographical "synods" (they did not use the word); they thus became the first movement within the Reformation to establish a Protestant church order. In these meetings they expected God to lead them through his Spirit in a peculiar way and testified that this expectation was not disappointed (cf. Schleitheim).

It also follows from this visibility of the Christian body that it has the resources for its own continuity. So it was that this mainstream Anabaptism was the only form of dissenting Christianity to survive beyond 1540, and the only form of Protestantism able in that century to live without the support of the state (with the one exception of the later Huguenots).

V. The Church Is Missionary

Franklin Littell in his *The Anabaptist View of the Church* (reprinted in paperback as *The Origins of Sectarian Protestantism*) has demonstrated how central to the life of the early Anabaptist congregations was their conviction of missionary responsibility. The missionary character of the church was in the first place built into the Anabaptist understanding of their place in society as demonstrated by the practice of believer's baptism. If infants are to be baptized, then the church survives and expands predominantly by the preservation of a given social group. If the membership of the church is limited to those who have committed themselves through baptism upon confession of faith, then in every generation the survival of the church depends upon evangelism. Whether it be the winning of the children of believers or of those outside of Christian families, the missionary character of the church's appeal to the individual is the same.

This missionary character was furthered by the Anabaptist rejection of ties between church and state. According to the pattern followed by the Reformation, finally written into law in 1555, described by the slogan, "*cujus regio, ejus religio*," each province was already Christian and the kind of Christianity represented there was to be determined by the prince or the city council. Any need or responsibility for missionary activity was thereby undercut. The rejection of this geographic identification of the church made it both psychologically possible and morally binding upon the Anabaptists to consider all of Europe their missionary field.

This missionary mentality was furthered in addition by the rejection of the fixed financial support methods for the clergy. Most of the Roman Catholic clergy were supported by endowment funds, i.e., by interest upon land belonging to church agencies. The Reformers, even though they considered the practice of lending at interest to be unbiblical, did not change this pattern of ministerial support, except in some cases where the endowment funds were passed through the state treasuries or where the minister was directly supported from the government treasury. In either case, the ministry was thereby tied to local government and subservient to the controls of each state unit. While retaining serious respect for the function of the local resident ministry in each congregation (cf. Schleitheim), the Anabaptists placed their emphasis upon the itinerant evangelist who, following the pattern of those sent out by Jesus, was supported only by the contributions of Christians. His reason for constant mobility was not only the biblical example but obviously the fact of persecution as well.

Behind all of this we should note yet a deeper insight into the nature of the Christian church. If the church is to be missionary, she must somehow also come to grips with the fact that her status is that of a minority. The nature of Christian commitment as a free and uncompelled decision makes practically certain that in any given time and place only a minority of the population will be committed Christian disciples. The Anabaptists saw the transition of the Christian church, especially in the fourth and fifth centuries AD to identity with society, as the "fall of the church." By this they meant not only the establishment of direct relationships to the state, though that was certainly one of the key changes in the fourth century. Nor did they mean only the entrance into the church of sub-Christian standards and patterns of worship, church organization, and piety, although such matters (the papacy, the mass, the worship of saints) were also quite important. But behind both of these there was the fundamental shift in the understanding of the church's place in the world; no longer seeing herself as a missionary minority, the church became herself one of the "powers that be," practically identical in membership with the society of Western Europe. It was this "fall" from which the Anabaptist movement sought to restore the church, not in a childish imitation of the New Testament congregational life, but in the recovery of the stance of the missionary minority.

VI. The Church Is a Brotherhood

In the actual beginnings of the congregation in Switzerland, discussion of the renewal of the Lord's Supper was prior to discussion of baptism. The Anabaptists were not only the first to establish, through the practice of baptism, a specifically Protestant movement; they were also the first Protestants, by the regular practice of communion service instead of merely an expurgated mass, to establish ordered Protestant congregational life. George Blaurock, when asked to identify himself to the police, was proud to say that it was he who had "restored the Lord's table and baptism." The Anabaptist view of the church is concerned, therefore, not simply with watching over the gate of membership (baptism); its concern is equally the maintenance of living fellowship, of which the frequent practice of the Lord's Supper is the symbolic and the real expression.

The practice of spiritual discipline following the "rule of Christ" (Matt 18:15) is prerequisite to the celebration of the Lord's Supper. It is thus made clear that the function of discipline is the maintenance of unity, and that this dimension of its significance is more profound than the mere keeping of the rule.

It was really only an expression of the true meaning of the shared supper when some Anabaptists moved all the way into full economic community and the common purse. The difference between the communitarian Anabaptists of Moravia and those of other parts of Europe which maintained private property has been overdrawn. Also the western Anabaptists considered the personal property of every individual as being available to the brotherhood in case of need, and the term "community of goods" was also frequently used by them to describe their position, even though it was not expressed through the form of the common purse.

We should see a further expression of the brotherhood character of the church in a concern which the Anabaptists, almost alone in their time, had for the renewal of Christian unity. In spite of the fact that they were being persecuted by the various Catholic and Protestant governments of German-speaking Europe, they repeatedly came back to the authorities, especially during the first thirty years, saying, "If you call yourselves Christians you must be willing to discuss with us what it is you hold against us, and to read the scripture together with us." There was thus no acceptance of the dividedness of the several Christian groups.

VII. The Church Is Led by the Word and the Spirit

Under this general title we bring together a number of themes related to the authority of Scripture and to the place of the Holy Spirit in the life of the early Anabaptist churches.

A. Primitivism

Franklin Littell has given currency to this label as describing the Anabaptist intention to "restore" the life of the church according to New Testament patterns. Leaning on more recent phenomena within American churches, most strikingly expressed within the Disciples' tradition, Littell ascribes to this idea of "restoration" a naive character, as if the Anabaptists thought they were in some childish sense imitating every detail of the life of the New Testament authority in church life. Their concern was not for the childishness or simplicity with which the New Testament could be read to find in it full answers and fixed patterns; but they were concerned that the Bible, and especially the New Testament, be taken as authoritative *in whatever is clearly enjoined,* whether by precept or by example. They did not say that everything in the life of the church must be done exactly as it was done in the New Testament; but they did object to ecclesiastical prescriptions which insisted that things must be done *differently* from the early church (cf. Conrad Grebel in 1523).

B. The Spirit and the Word

For the Anabaptists there could be no opposition between Scripture as an authority, to be found speaking in the text itself, and the appropriation of its meanings through subjective conviction as the work of the Holy Spirit. The two were for them inseparable. When in the second generation they could be found writing tracts about "The Inner and the Outer Word," the point was to insist that these two dimensions of revelation must not be separated.

It is striking that the critics of the Anabaptists attempted to attack them from both sides because of this unity with which they combined inner and outer authority. Some, notably Huldrych Zwingli, considered the Anabaptists to be "enthusiasts," claiming special revelation independent of Scripture. His successor, Bullinger, had the opposite objection: namely, that the Anabaptists stuck too closely to the letter of Scripture rather than accepting the "interpretations" by which he could make a case for the state church, for infant baptism, for the sword and the oath.

Over against the fanatics like David Joris or the prophets at Münster, the mainstream Anabaptists insisted upon the priority of biblical revelation as sole ultimate standard; over against magisterial orthodoxy, for which the proper teaching of correct doctrines was a sufficient guarantee of truth, they insisted upon the necessity of personal understanding, acceptance, commitment, and congregational involvement, refusing precisely the opposition between these two dimensions which was shared by their attackers on both sides.

C. The Old Testament and the New

For the Reformers, the total Bible was to be taken as one flat book, with every text having the same kind of authority, regardless of its place in the Bible, when it served their purposes. The religious government of the Old Testament could be an example for the state church in the sixteenth century without reference to what happened to that government under divine providence in the Old Testament or what Jesus did about being a king. On the other hand, the Reformers did develop a "canon within the canon" as an interpretive guide, seen most clearly in Martin Luther's ability to evaluate everything by whether it corresponded with his doctrine of justification by faith alone.

The Anabaptists were the only mission group of the Reformation to make clear the fundamental distinction between the Old Testament and the New. Thus the "canon within the canon" is the relationship of promise and fulfilment which modern theology calls *"heilsgeschichte"*: the idea that there is a movement within God's purposes which brings the biblical witness to its high point in the work of Jesus himself, and which sees his continuing work in the life of a disciple people. Over against the "mainstream magisterial" Reformation for which in all history there has been but one age since the covenant with Abraham, and over against the fanatical reformers who were sure that the third age of world history was beginning in their own person, the Anabaptists spoke only of the Old Covenant and the New, thus safeguarding the centrality of the incarnation against both the pre-Christian dimensions of the Old Testament and the anti-Christian claimants to new revelation.

The significance of the relationship between Testaments is enormous in practical consequences; nonresistance, the swearing of oaths, and believer's baptism are among them.

VIII. The Contemporary Theological Significance of the Anabaptist Vision

A. The Problems Are Still the Same

In spite of total difference in detail, it can easily be argued that the fundamental issues facing Christians in our day are no different from those to which the Anabaptists were responding. In spite of all the changes, we still live as they did in a world with a background of "Christianized" conformity, which gives to the search for renewal a fate not much different from that which it had in their day.

The *obstacles* to renewal are still, as then, Constantinianism in its confusion of the church with society at large, and the willingness to use in the service of the church the tools of this world (the alliance to the state). The *internal test* before which the renewal of the church will succeed or fail is still whether or not there shall be a redemptive yet binding personal discipline, and whether it can include the economic realm. The *external test* of the church's faithfulness is still today, as then, her moral independence of the state and her rejection of war, and whether she has a missionary method and motivation.

All of this is reflected in the fact that now as then, the central issues in Christian faithfulness are not those of orthodoxy with regard to a doctrine of Scripture or salvation, but rather the questions of ecclesiology (the church), eschatology (the Christian hope for history), and ethics. These are the fundamental points at which the Anabaptists differed from the "mainstream" of their time and where Christian faithfulness will differ as well today.

B. Some Are Ready to Hear

From a number of perspectives we find on the theological scene a new kind of openness to this witness. Especially in Europe, churchmen realize that they have come to the end of the age of Constantine. They are now able to look back on the Middle Ages and the Reformation, rejecting in principle the use of the methods of persecution and the bondage of the church to the state. This ability to reevaluate their own history has been made more objective thanks to the contribution of theological liberalism. Europe also has, as a result of the experience of two world wars, a deeper sense than there is in North America of the breakdown of traditional Christendom.

Another dimension of this openness is the discovery by numerous contemporary theologians of the biblical doctrine of the church as clearly something other than simply the religious dimension of a total society. We find this in different ways, in Barth, Brunner, ecumenical theology, and biblical theology.

Still another dimension of the rediscovery of this vision of the disciples' church comes from the mission field. It is from that perspective that it has been seen again that the church is a visible body, a minority, and a group with a mission to the larger society.

On the level of theory, openness to this vision has been furthered by the work of social historians like Troeltsch and Sweet, who have corrected the history writing of the Reformation by demonstrating that the free church tradition is itself an independent and valid option, needing to be respected in its own rights rather than decried as having opposed the mainstream Reformers. Within this world of scholarship, it must be said as well that the quality of research going into Anabaptist studies in the last two generations has won for this heritage a new appreciation.

XI. Anabaptism vs. Mennonites

We must conclude our study by bringing back together the two realities with which the study began: on the one hand actual North American Mennonitism in the process of coming out of its ethnic and cultural isolation; on the other the Anabaptist vision as more clearly understood thanks to recent scholarship.

The first conclusion which must be clearly stated is that present Mennonitism must not be identified with the Anabaptist vision as if it were that vision which was leading its development. From 1930 to 1945, beginning with the scholarly work of Harold S. Bender and coming to the end of a stage with the end of Civilian Public Service, it could be said that the institutional developments of Mennonite colleges and the Mennonite Central Committee were sincerely thought of as an expression and an instrument of the Anabaptist vision. Since then it has, however, become increasingly clear that most of the developments among the Mennonites who have sought education and moved to the city have not by and large demonstrated a primarily missionary motivation; the conscientious objection of Mennonite young men has not demonstrated primarily and purely a commitment to suffering love; the growth of Mennonite institutions has not been solely with a vision of cultural discrimination and missionary mobility.

Anabaptism was intended in the sixteenth century as a corrective. It never claimed to be more than "the rest of the Reformation." It never sought separation from the larger stream of Protestant Reformation and was driven into separate congregational identity only by the failure of the Reformation in its larger forms to be faithful in overcoming its subservience to the state. Thus, those who represent the Anabaptist vision should be open to welcome every possible occasion to feed their corrective witness back into the mainstream of Christian thought. Such a witness cannot by definition serve to justify the self-centeredness and separate identity of a denomination.

Insofar as we confess the Anabaptist vision to be, as far as we can see and to those items to which it speaks, biblical, and our own commitment, we are not justified but rather judged by it. Mennonitism in its seventeenth- to nineteenth-century form by ceasing to be missionary became a mass church of its own. We can condemn Catholicism for being a mass church; but at least Catholic theologians have the honesty to recognize this is their position. When the "believers' church" becomes the contrary of that and continues to fly the old flag, the condemnation is greater.

Similarly, contemporary Mennonitism after emerging from cultural separateness has lost as much as it has gained of Anabaptist insight. The professionalizing of ministerial leadership, the development of the power and wealth of church institutions without an immediate congregational base or a congregational procedure of reaching decisions, the resulting increase in denominational separateness and self-sufficiency, the decrease in congregational responsibility and congregational program and discipline are all moving Mennonites in North America away from the Anabaptist vision, even though some of the developments have taken place under the flag of Anabaptism.

After having struggled in the first place for a degree of self-understanding and perhaps even self-justification from the rediscovery of their historic rootage, Mennonites now find themselves placed before an unexpected kind of challenge. The historical meaning of Anabaptism, which is biblically justified, is not identical with but in serious conflict with contemporary Mennonitism. We thus must move on beyond historical reconstructions to a far more profound repentance and renewal, recommitting ourselves to that vision, being judged by it and thereby being justified by it in spite of our cultural inferiority and our separateness; or else we must face the difference between that vision and our present existence and conclude honestly that out of faithfulness to the Anabaptist vision the Mennonite denomination should cease to exist.

2

The Mennonite Conception of the Church and Its Relation to Community Building[1]

Harold S. Bender

In the sense in which we Mennonites understand the meaning of the words "Church" and "Christian" we might well substitute "church" for "community" in the title of our conference on "Mennonite Community Life." For have we not historically, and in our highest thought, always held that to be "Christian" means to follow Christ in *all* our ways including what the world calls "secular," and that the "church" is a brotherhood of love in which all the members minister to each other in all their needs *both* temporal and spiritual? And what more is a Christian community than a fellowship of disciples of Christ sharing a common faith, and under a common Lord helping one another achieve the fullness of abundant life which the Savior came to bring? Nevertheless, inasmuch as our traditional thought of the church commonly concerns itself more directly with the preaching of the gospel and the provision of a ministry of worship and spiritual edification, whereas our traditional thought of community directs itself more to those interests and activities which are not primarily or narrowly religious such as economic, social, and cultural, it may be well to retain the distinction of the two terms.

[1]. Reprinted from *The Mennonite Quarterly Review* 19.2 (1945).

In agreeing to such a distinction, however, may I voice the devout hope that our discussions in this conference may help us to eliminate from our minds the dangerously unscriptural and un-Mennonite duality by which we so often draw a line between sacred and secular, between church and community. In drawing such a line we fall under the influence of three erroneous types of thought—Roman Catholic, popular Protestant, and plain worldly. Since the early Middle Ages Catholicism has taught that only that way of life is sacred which devotes itself wholly to narrowly religious duties and forsakes the common life of man; thus, those persons are sacred who enter the celibate life of the clergy or of the monkish orders, and those things only are sacred which are used in the ritual of worship; the common life of man, in home and family, in vocation and culture, is secular and of a lower order. Popular Protestantism from a different point of view has sanctified only certain limited areas of life, particularly the inward experience of salvation and fellowship with Christ, and has abandoned large areas of the common life to compromise with the prevailing un-Christian world order on the specious plea that they cannot be Christianized in a world such as we live in. Out of this popular Protestant point of view has come the strange doctrine which some among us have not altogether escaped, that such great biblical teachings as sanctification and holiness refer rather to states of mind than to achievements of living in obedience to Christ. Our modern pagan world, from again another point of view, has also been all too glad to confine religion to the formal aspects of worship chiefly inside of church buildings, and claim the rest of life for its secular self. What has religion to do with philosophy, science, politics, government, social service work, literature, art, etc., we are admonished.

For five hundred years our Western civilization has increasingly made good this claim and under the leadership of an increasingly irreligious upper class has wrested area after area of the common life from the control of the Christian church and its dominant influence. It has so secularized our world that millions of men and women now get along from birth to death without ever touching religion or the church in any aspect of their life—marriage, birth, death, education, health, money, recreation, literature, art, occupation. Thus, the whole of life has become devoid of any sense of divine calling or claim, or any awareness of eternal values and destiny. From this tragic secularization we are reaping a dreadful harvest and shall reap even worse. Some of us, in our haste to protect the church from contaminating itself by contact with this modern world of unbelief, and from losing its supreme mission, that of bringing Christ to a lost world, have fallen into the trap of this modern secularism by too hastily condemning as "social gospel" or "social service" the extension of Christian witness and service into unoccupied needy areas of the common life, forgetting that in denying the Christian church the right of entrance into these fields we are actually consigning much of life to condemnation as secular, as not intended for Christian occupation. Such hasty name-calling should be classed as aid and comfort to the enemy of souls who must be only too happy to have Christians concentrate on their inner life and leave the real life of daily duty and experience to the domination of our contemporary pagan culture. To be sure, all these so-called secular activities and vocations such as education, hospital and medical service, relief work, cooperatives, special work, can be wholly secularized, and they usually are in our modern world, without any thought of Christian calling or witness to the gospel. But they can also be conducted to the glory of God and the extension of his kingdom, the saving of souls and the upbuilding of the church. Whether these things are sacred or secular does not lie objectively in the activities; it lies in the spirit, purpose, and character of the actor, the man or woman in the work. Think, for instance, of how such Mennonite hospitals as those at La Junta and Newton have been made thoroughly Christian institutions in spite of the fact that many hospitals are purely secular. To the early Anabaptists and Mennonites, none of these areas of activity that were at all possible for the Christian were counted secular; all were sacred, to be alone as to the Lord.

Let us then not be modernized after the fashion of the Catholic, popular Protestant, or pagan worldly man; let us hold fast to our Scriptural and historic heritage on this point. What we cannot make sacred we have no business doing at all. If we cannot build Christian communities, we have no business being a part of any community. Business is not business, it is life, and life must be Christian. If business cannot be Christianized, then let the Christian get out of it. In either case, whether Christianizing a particular area of life, or getting the Christian out of it, the church, according to the Mennonite conception, is mightily concerned, and must furnish vision, guidance, assistance, and if need be, control.

But it may be asked, what bearing has this on our theme? Just this: we cannot assess the bearing of our conception of the church on the present needs, unless we know first what basic conception of Christianity lies behind it. If Christianity to us means primarily an inner experience, and flight from the workaday realities of life into a dream world of emotionalized religious forms and sentiment, then the church will probably turn out to be for us primarily a resource agency for the promotion of individual "piety." We will "go to church" on Sunday or on prayer meeting night, and cultivate the garden of God within our individual souls while the garden of our daily life will be cultivated with different machinery, with the help of the state, cultural association, community organizations, even corporations, etc., or allowed to grow up in weeds. Then there will be no Christian community, and such a conference as this will be a waste of time and money. Since, however, the Mennonite rejects this view of Christianity, and holds that to be Christian means to bring the whole of life under the obedience of Christ, even every thought into captivity to him, then the church, which is the fellowship of disciples, will be the chief means by which he will cultivate the garden of his outward daily life as well as the inward garden of his soul.

May we now consider the cardinal elements in the Mennonite conception of the church. They are eight, and each one of them has a bearing on our present-day needs and on community building. (There are other aspects of the church and its work, of course, which are not noted here.)

1. The Concept of the Church as the Body of Christ

This is drawn directly from such New Testament passages as Rom 12, 1 Cor 12, and Eph 4. All the members of the church together constitute a life unity of which Christ is the directing and controlling head, and are therefore under his authority; how can then can a member of Christ live any part of his life outside of his control? If we are members of his body, does only our heart belong to him, while our hands and feet or our head may be left out in the world? At the same time, the members of his body are all members one of another; they share a common life and work; they have obligations to one another. The New Testament does not say that they are members of one another only on Sunday, or at prayer meeting, or at the communion table and the feet-washing tub. This body of Christ is always a body, always continuously functioning as a unit. Here is the primary basis for Christian community. How can we dissolve the body of Christ at the close of the benediction on Sunday morning and live the remaining days of the week as though each life unto himself separately? Or are we after all only a collection of individuals, each worshiping God in his own heart and looking after the salvation of his own soul only?

This historic concept is well expressed by the refusal of our Swiss, German, and Dutch forefathers to use the term "church" or "*Kirche*" in referring to the brotherhood, insisting on the term "*Gemeinde*," the term used in the German Bible. "*Kirche*" they used to refer to the great state churches whether Protestant or Catholic. "*Gemeinde*" (there is no good English equivalent) was the proper name for the body of Christ, the fellowship of true believers. As long as the German language was used among us in America this practice was continued. Only with the adoption of English have we come to speak of ourselves as a church. The German Bible, in fact, never uses the word "*Kirche*" to apply to the Body of Christ, but always "*Gemeinde*." The force of "*Gemeinde*" is exactly that of body or community, a group of people who share a common life. Have we unconsciously adopted another unscriptural and un-Mennonite concept of the church as we have taken over the English name?

2. The Concept of the Church as the Temple of God

This concept is drawn from Eph 2:22 where the church is called an habitation of God through the Spirit; and from 1 Cor 3 where Paul says: "Know ye not that ye are the temple of God, and that the Spirit of God dwelleth in you? If any man defiles the temple of God, him shall God destroy: for the temple of God is holy, which temple ye are." The defiling of the temple of God of which Paul here speaks is the divisive, schismatic spirit which was so evident at Corinth. The realization that the entire church, not only the individual member, is the dwelling place of God, is to curb strife and schism and conserve the unity of the church. The presence of God in the church hallows the fellowship of believers, reminds them of their holy calling, rekindles the fires of flickering love, and knits hearts together in the bonds of peace. Only the church can have this sense of the presence of God; no secular organization can call on this resource to meet the constant threat of organizational breakdown or divisive factionalism. What community does not need help to meet the strains and stresses which accompany every attempt of frail human personalities to build a common life in cooperative endeavor! But what community can have the help of God like the Christian church! When our 1944 General Conference was in a period of strain and tension, and some of the seams threatened to open, it was coming humbly into the presence of God, whose temple and dwelling place we were, that brought us the victory and prevented the temple from being defiled. This concept means much to true community building.

3. The Concept of the Church as a Brotherhood

"Brother" and "Sister" are scriptural designations for members of the church which have become conventional with us and have largely lost their meaning. But in the New Testament they have a powerful force. They indicate that the members of the church are so closely bound together by ties of love and mutual concern that they think of and act toward each other as members of a great family of whom God is the Father and Christ the Elder Brother. They also suggest that in the church there are no classes, no clergy and laity, no artificial distinctions, but a fellowship of equals. When "Reverend," "Doctor," "Bishop," "Professor," or any other such forms replace the simple brother and sister greeting among us in the church, we shall be well on the way to losing this concept of the church as a brotherhood and its powerful motivation for Christian community life. The great state churches and denominations of ancient and modern times were not and are not brotherhoods but great institutional machines operated by and controlled by a professional class of clergy, theologians, and administrators, who do many things *"for"* the members, but in which the vast mass of the membership have little share in the government, activity, life, and service of the church and in which there is accordingly no true common life. In such an ecclesiastical machine the sense of brotherhood perishes, the desire for community vanishes, and the very basis for effective community building disappears. There is even a sense in which the resistance of the Mennonite church of times past to the designation of its ministers as "pastors" was a healthy sign; active healthy members of the church do not need pastors, they need leaders, and servants. "One is your master, even Christ, and all ye are brethren." When true Christian brotherhood exists, then all the resources of every member will be enlisted for the common work of the church and to meet the several needs of all. This is community.

4. The Concept of the Church as a Body Separated from the World

The New Testament plainly teaches that the disciple of Christ is in the world but not of it, that he can have no fellowship with the unfruitful works of darkness, that he cannot be yoked with unbelievers, that he is a stranger and a pilgrim, that his citizenship is in heaven. This implies that the individual disciple of Christ will make a clean break with the world, i.e., with contemporary society, in all those ways of life which would invalidate his discipleship (and he will find that these ways are many). But we also read that the people of God as a whole, the entire church, is constituted a holy nation, a chosen race, a people belonging peculiarly to God. In other words, the church as a body makes a break with the world and operates as a distinct social group dedicated to God. This concept is further fortified by the teaching that when men are born again from above, and come out of darkness into light, they are invited to enter the church, i.e., to step out of one realm into another, "to be translated out of the power of darkness into the Kingdom of the Son of His love." What does all this mean if not that the church is essentially separated from the world order of which it is externally a part? Now this separation from the world, both for the individual Christian and for the whole church, is not merely an artificial protective device to help weak Christians better to meet the enemy or to keep out of temptation, but rather an expression of fundamental reality. The Christian separates himself because he cannot find a home in the world. He is a child of light how can he live in the darkness? He is naturally separated. He does not, accordingly, detach himself with painful hesitation from the worldly society about him, casting back over his shoulder regretful Lot's wife looks, but rather marvels that any Christian should hanker after the fellowship of the world or find happiness in any form in its company.

The significance of the separation concept for Christian community building is obvious. The members of the church are gathered out of the society of which they are externally a part and break off connections with many of its activities and persons because of the divergence in ethical and religious standards. Thus, any real community with the unbelieving world becomes impossible. Where then shall the Christian go to find the satisfaction of his various needs for which he is dependent upon others—whether vocational, economic, cultural, social, or spiritual? He must go to those who share his standards, and who are devoted to the same goal, who have the same Lord. Here he can find unclouded fellowship and happy communion; here he can enter into cooperative activities without fear; here he can leave his burdens with the assurance that love will bear them with him; here he can share in perfect community all that he has and is.

5. The Concept of the Church as a Disciplinary Body

I hesitate very much to use the term "disciplinary body" here and do so only for want of a better term. In so doing, I do not think of a "punitive body," which, alas, is what so many both among the laity and the ministry seem to mean by discipline, contrary to the New Testament teaching. I think rather of a restorative body, which, by the various means of grace at its disposal, builds up the weak, restores the fallen, heals the broken and wounded, strengthens the feeble knees, encourages the fainthearted, equips with weapons those who are unarmed for the fight, knits the hearts of all together in love. Now such discipline, wisely directed by skilled leaders, is a tremendous source of strength for the individual and in turn for the entire body. It contributes to stability, sturdiness, and defensive strength, building up also resources for offensive activity and for all kinds of ministry. It undergirds the entire body with a cohesive unity which vastly multiplies the strength of the individual. All this is obviously a great contribution to true community building. The functioning of the church as a disciplinary body may, however, also become a source of weakness, particularly if the discipline is unintelligent or punitive, or consists primarily of the exercise of authority by one individual over others. Brotherhood and community are destroyed when one of the brethren lords it over God's heritage, even if he holds the highest office of the church. This danger has plagued the Mennonite Church throughout its history; but it need not be so, for it is only the abuse of true scriptural discipline and not the use of it which leads to such tragic consequences.

6. The Concept of the Suffering Church

Our Anabaptist forefathers understood full well that when they assumed the responsibility of full obedience to Christ, they would find themselves in conflict with the world round about them, and that this conflict would lead to suffering. But this did not deter them; it rather drew them closer together in mutual sympathy and strengthening of heart. The fellowship of suffering fortified them for the conflict, and the sense of the common enemy made them realize their interdependence upon one another in faith and prayer and mutual aid. Out of the crucible of tribulation and hardship came a depth of fellow-feeling and love which never would have come out of a life that was only one of ease. Thereby the sense of community was greatly intensified. Have we not also felt this drawing together in times of need and danger? Our hearts go out to each other when suffering and loss become the lot of any one individual, family, or congregation. Truly the concept of the suffering church increases the strength of our community foundations.

7. The Concept of the Church as a Witness to the Gospel

Another New Testament concept of the church which has been precious to us as Mennonites is that the church in its total redeemed life must be a testimony of the grace and power of God, a witness to the meaning of the gospel and a source of attraction to the sinner. The full message of the good news of the kingdom of God cannot be made clear to a lost world unless the corporate life of the believers shows forth the excellencies of the Savior. "Ye are the light of the world, ye are the salt of the earth, let your light so shine before men that they may see your good works and glorify your Father." All of these "ye's" and "your's" are plural, not singular, and were addressed to a company of disciples. One disciple can do something but not much. Nor is the increased witnessing power of the body primarily due to the multiplication of numbers. It is rather that there are aspects of the gospel, of the kingdom, of the righteousness of God, which cannot be manifested in individuals alone but require the life of a group, in which right relationships of man to man can be expressed. The whole church must display the character and will of God in all its living. There must be a holy society, a godly family life, a Christian community, to express the fullness of the abundant life which Christ came to bring.

8. The Concept of the Church as the Final Goal of All Christian Work

In Eph 5 the apostle Paul tells us that "Christ gave himself for the church that he might present it to himself a glorious church not having spot or wrinkle or any such thing; but that it should be holy and without blemish." In the third chapter he pledges that the church will give "glory to God by Christ Jesus throughout all ages, world without end." In this concept of the church we have a vision of the ultimate goal of Christ's redemptive work—a glorious, holy, spotless body which will continue throughout all the ages. Christ's goal must also be our goal. We too must seek to present to our Lord at the end of time this glorious church as the best possible church. We are not only concerned with saving individuals but with saving the whole company of the redeemed as an organic fellowship of the saints, living a corporate life which is conformed to her Lord. This striving for a pure church has been deeply imbedded in our Mennonite thought from the very beginning, and it is deeply scriptural. It has delivered us from an excessive individualism and given us a vision which will challenge us to the end of time, and which requires that the total life of the brotherhood be sanctified. Here again we have another basis for community building.

This brief review of the eight cardinal elements in the Mennonite concept of the church—the vision of the church as a body of Christ, as the dwelling place of God, as a brotherhood of love, as separated from the world, as a disciplinary body, as a suffering church, as a witness to the gospel, and as the final goal of all Christian work, gives us a vision of a holy community with a common life, dedicated to God, knit together in a marvelous way, the object of all our striving and our dreams. Such a church is magnificently equipped, by the grace of God, to meet present-day needs in a twentieth-century world. Christian community life will be the inevitable expression of its inner nature, whether locally or on a broad scale. And Christian community life will in turn be a tower of strength to the church in its total service in the kingdom of God.

Significant consequences for our ethical and social thinking result from the Mennonite conception of the church as delineated above.

1. In the first place this concept of the church leads the Christian to withdraw his major energies from active participation in the general program of world betterment and attempted reconstruction of the entire non-Christian world order and focus them on the building of the Christian community. His hope for the world is the church and the creation of a Christian social order within the fellowship of the church brotherhood. Extension of this Christian order is by the conversion of individuals and their transfer out of the world into the church will be his method of working at saving the world; it is the method Christ and the apostles used; it is the method of the Anabaptist fathers.

2. In the second place, it is within the church as a brotherhood of love that the fullness of the Christian life ideal is to be expressed. This means that what is commonly thought of as *church life* is greatly enriched in quality and extended in scope. Many things will be included within the church which may seem to some to be secular. In the true sense the church becomes the Christian community.

3. In the third place the provision of this enriched and extended life will require the service of large numbers of what for want of a better term we call lay members. The ministers being limited in number and having the all-important and primary function of preaching the gospel and declaring the whole counsel of God cannot and should not provide this service, not because they would need to "stoop" to do so, but simply because they cannot do everything and should not rob the laity of their part. Unfortunately, in recent years we have been inclined to violate this principle.

4. In the fourth place we find that the nature of the church brings with it into our community building program a powerful sense of belonging together, of needing each other, of receiving from and giving to each other, that is of great value in Christian community building. But we also see that this feeling requires expression in many and various forms in Christian community life if the full content of the Christian experience and the meaning of the church is to be satisfied.

Thus, in the light of his church concept, the Mennonite is both pessimistic and optimistic about this world. He does not agree with the Catholic and the Calvinist, who hold that the world as it is can be redeemed as a whole; nor with the social gospeller, humanitarian, or evolutionist who hold that it can be gradually transformed into an ideal world of righteousness, peace, and social perfection. On the other hand he does not agree with the Lutheran and many Fundamentalists that it is impossible to do the will of God and obey the teachings of Christ in the present evil world and that therefore we must compromise by participating in the evils of a sub-Christian social order. The Mennonite believes rather that the kingdom of God can be and should be set up within the fellowship of the church here and now and lived out to its fullest meaning. The world may be full of evils, as Luther says in his great hymn, but the life within the Christian brotherhood community is satisfyingly full of victory, peace, love, and joy.

3

The Anabaptist Theology of Discipleship[1]

Harold S. Bender

It is perhaps unwise and even futile to attempt to find the central controlling idea of Anabaptist theology, particularly in view of the general absence of speculative and systematizing thought among Anabaptist writers, but I, with no doubt others among our guild of Mennonite theologians and historians, am as yet unwilling to abandon the attempt. The paper which I now submit for your consideration represents a continuance of the search for the answer to this question.

In my first endeavor to distill the essence of Anabaptist theology, the results of which are recorded in *The Anabaptist Vision,* written in 1944, I proposed three basic elements in the Anabaptist vision, a new concept of the church as a brotherhood of committed believers, a new concept of the essence of Christianity as discipleship, and a new ethic of love. So far as I am aware, no criticism of this analysis has been offered thus far, except that by Prof. Don Smucker in his *The Mennonite Quarterly Review* article entitled, "Anabaptist Historiography in the Scholarship of Today." Smucker there criticized me for having omitted the great Anabaptist emphasis on the authority of the Scripture. I agree that this important concept in Anabaptist theology should have been included in some form. My defense for omitting it from the Anabaptist Vision would be, (1) that it is a formal concept, and

---

[1]. Reprinted from *The Mennonite Quarterly Review* 24.1 (1950).

(2) that it is not distinctive of Anabaptism. Not only did all the reformers hold to "*sola scriptura*," but all historic evangelical Protestantism has ever since held to it. The uniqueness of Anabaptism lies not in its loyalty to Scripture as the sole and sufficient source and authority for faith and life, but in its attitude to the content of Scripture. True, Anabaptism was not fully conformant to Reformation Protestantism, in that it refused to place the Old Testament on a parity with the New Testament, choosing rather to make the new covenant of Christ supreme and relegating therefore the Old Testament to the position of a preparatory instrument in God's program. This important basic attitude toward the two testaments has significant theological consequences, with its bearing on the concept of the church (e.g., the church is not composed of entire families, or peoples as in the case of God's people in the Old Testament, but regenerated individuals, and baptism is not the counterpart of circumcision therefore), as well as on ethical questions such as the state and nonresistance. The thorough study of the Anabaptist attitude toward Scripture which we greatly need has not yet been done. It would be particularly helpful in our time, when under the influence of general orthodox Protestant thought, as well as modern Fundamentalism, some among us are inclined to give the Old Testament too high a place, with undesirable consequences in the field of ethics (nonresistance), as well as in important points in the doctrine of the church and in eschatology. But the Anabaptist doctrine of Scripture does not seem to me to give us the answer to the question we are asking regarding the central regulative idea or ideas of Anabaptism, important as it is to understand fully and correctly this idea.

For a time I thought, with others, who perhaps still think so, that the central controlling idea of Anabaptism was the concept of the church. It seemed so clear that the Swiss Brethren and the Dutch "Menists," beginning with Conrad Grebel and Menno Simons, made their great goal the establishment of the true church. This was the primary challenge of Grebel, Manz, and Stumpf to Zwingli in those days in 1523 and 1524, and 1525, when the whole course of the Swiss Reformation was being decided. "Establish the true church according to the Apostles and we will go with you and we shall have success," was the great call of the first Anabaptists, not only to Zwingli, but to all the Reformers of their day; and when the answer came back, "No, we cannot risk the separated, committed believers' and disciples' church but must continue the mass institutional church," the break was inevitable.

The vision of the true church which had come so often before to earnest Christians down through the centuries after the fall of Christianity under Constantine, could not be surrendered; this time, in the great new day, it would be realized. And from that day to this it has been increasingly realized (more in form than in essence, I admit), in the great free church movement of Anglo-Saxon-American Christendom. Certainly this is a major powerful concept, and this vision of this true church of Christ has been the gleam which we Mennonites have always followed, and which in its pervasive form of narrow legalistic sect-building has been perhaps the greatest tragedy and destructive factor in our history. Yet, with all its power and historic significance it seems to me not to be the ultimate idea. In a sense, is not the concept of the church also a formal concept? The character of the church is determined by something beyond the church itself, for it ultimately derives from the concept of the nature of the Christian experience and the Christian life. The concept of the church is actually a derivative idea. We have not yet arrived at the heart when we stop with the church, even though the Anabaptist concept of the church is certainly one of the most distinctive features of Anabaptist theology.

There are some who would have us believe, in the third place, that the concept of love, or in its narrower applied form, nonresistance, is the central idea of Anabaptism. Now all Christians believe in love, hence this could be a distinctive concept for Anabaptism only if it is a particular type of love, or applied in some unique way, or directed toward some unique object. This is not the case in Anabaptism. Much as I believe in the importance of the ethic of love in the Anabaptist vision, I must dissent from those who would make it the regulative concept of our faith. Nonresistance does flow from the concept of love as the Anabaptist sees it, but not so in the understanding of other Protestants nor of Catholics. Nonresistance arises rather, either from the basic rejection of force and violence, or the concept of the sacredness of human life, or the plain command of Christ. In the last analysis the meaning of love for the Anabaptist flows from the understanding of the nature and example of Jesus.

Does it not seem that every time we have sought the essence of Anabaptism in one of the other major ideas, such as the Scripture, the church, or the principle of love, we are driven a step further into the ultimate relationship of the individual Christian to Christ? I would therefore propose that we pursue our search further down this road, for I believe that if we do so we shall find the answer in the concept of discipleship as the most characteristic, most central, most essential and regulative concept in Anabaptist thought, which largely determines all else. We shall also find at this point the parting of the ways between various forms of Christianity, and various types of theology and ethics.

What think ye of Christ? The limits of this paper will not admit of a comprehensive review of all the answers which have been given in Christian history and theology to this question. May I briefly sketch the major types of answer and then proceed to delineate the major features of the Anabaptist theology of discipleship.

First, there are those who think of Christ primarily as a prophet or moral teacher, one who brings intellectual truth out of which to build a system of thought, theological or ethical, with answers to the meaning of life or existence. For such Christ remains primarily an object of thought and reflection, about whom one intellectualizes. It goes with a certain attitude toward life in which all too often speculation, whether philosophical or theological, becomes the technique by which life is mastered. The actual processes of life are carried on often quite apart from the ideal of truth which Christ brings, and intellectualization or rationalization is used to close the gap or conceal the disparity between the comprehended ideal of Christ and the disobedient practice of the actual life. This is the peculiar danger of classic Protestant theology, particularly of Calvinism.

Another answer is to think of Christ primarily as a being to be worshiped. The most orthodox theology of his person as a member of the Trinity, is combined with a high liturgy of praise and symbolic representations in sacrament, in art, and in literature, which call forth the ultimate in adoration. This type may eventuate in a Christ-mysticism, or in a refined theological dialectics, or in sensualized liturgy and routine formalism. In any case Christ remains remote from the actual daily practice of life. This is the peculiar danger of Catholicism, Greek and Roman.

A third answer to Christ is to think of him and use him exclusively as Savior. Now in the true ultimate and comprehensive meaning of salvation this answer would lead us into the heart of the Anabaptist theology of discipleship. Actually it often stops far short of that, for Christ becomes only the sin-bearer, who by his atoning death on the cross delivers from the guilt of sin, and by forgiveness and justification reconciles the sinner to God and brings peace. This marvelous and wholly necessary experience of the forgiving and cleansing grace of God in Christ, both for the past sinful life and for the inevitable sins of believers, is intended in God's plan of salvation to be only the initial step in Christian experience as well as the constant carrying foundation for the daily life, not the whole of the Christian experience nor even its end goal. But the joy and blessing of this experience with the access it brings to God and the blessedness of the fellowship with Christ is so great, that all too often it becomes the essence and the whole of the Christian experience, beside which other things become relatively unimportant. Justification by faith becomes so great and so wonderful, that sanctification of life and obedience to Christ, and transformation after his image, are in effect minimized and neglected. The Lordship of Christ is in effect set aside. This has been the peculiar danger of historic Lutheranism and remains the besetting temptation of modern Fundamentalism. Dispensationalism even goes so far as to relegate the Lordship, or let us say, the Kingship of Christ to a later age beyond the scope and ken of our present Christian practice.

Then there is the final answer to Christ which takes him as everything, Prophet, Savior, *and Lord*, and makes the believer his disciple. This answer basically believes that Christ is to be translated in the life-expression of the disciple, or in the words of the apostle Paul, Christ is to be "formed" in him, and he is to be Lord of all his life. This is the Anabaptist answer to Christ, and out of the understanding of the meaning of this answer derive all the major ideas of Anabaptism. (It has been also in some sense the answer of other movements in the history of the church, including even Methodism and Pietism in its best form.)

Now the idea of discipleship is not unique with Anabaptism, for it has appeared in various forms through the Christian centuries, sometimes in almost identical form with that which it took in Anabaptism. It was the vision of the earliest Christians of the New Testament age. One of its purest expressions was in Peter Chelchitzki of Bohemia (1390–1460), spiritual father of the Unitas Fratrum. But though the ideal of "following Christ," "*die Nachfolge Christi*," or of "imitating" him, has been a recurring creative idea all through Christian history, it was the mission of the Anabaptists to give expression in a powerful way to this idea at a creative moment in history, at the beginning of our modern age in such a way that this time it did not die shortly but was incorporated in a continuing group, and through manifold ways fertilized modern Protestantism. The tragedy is that the very group that professed this vision and seriously attempted to practice it lost its witnessing zeal and ultimately no small amount of the reality of this vision in its own practice, so that the discipleship (which its theology still holds) became flabby and diluted or shriveled and lost much of its vitality, though still retaining much of its pristine character.

In essence the discipleship which the Anabaptists proclaimed was simply the bringing of the whole of life under the Lordship of Christ, and the transformation of this life, both personal and social, after his image. From this point of view they subjected not only the church but the whole social and cultural order to criticism; rejected what they found to be contrary to Christ, and attempted to put into actual practice his teachings as they understood them both ethically and sociologically.

Now anyone who undertakes such a critical examination of his own world, must disengage himself from the contemporary culture in which he is immersed in order to clearly discern the discrepancies between this culture and the Christ whom he wishes to express. Fortunately, the Anabaptists succeeded in doing this to a considerable extent, though in varying degree. They did not always succeed so well in the creative application of Christ to their situation, since they were early deprived of many of their better trained and more capable leaders with the necessary equipment of mind and heart, as well as experience plus courage, to undertake this tremendous task.

The Anabaptist theology of discipleship can be better and more fully understood perhaps by comparing it with two closely related types of conception and practice in the matter of following Christ; the first of these is the type of *Nachfolge Christi* so powerfully and so beautifully set forth by Thomas á Kempis about a century earlier in the book which next to the Bible itself has reputedly had a greater circulation and influence than any other book, *The Imitation of Christ*. For all its effectiveness in urging upon the Christian disciple the imitation of the character of his master by the conquest of the human passions and the vices to which they lead, and the production of the virtues of Christ, this book is concerned primarily with the inner world of the soul, where the believer is to cultivate the garden of his spiritual life with his eye constantly upon his ultimate personal goal, heaven. Self-renunciation and resignation are among the highest virtues. The reader is taught that only through suffering, by carrying his cross with him every day in imitation of Christ, can he reach the heavenly country. The goal of the disciple is purification of himself so that he can truly love God and Christ, and then also his neighbor. He is advised to avoid society as much as possible, to devote much time to contemplation, to read the "sacred writings" with his mind freed from temporal cares, and with devotion. Basically, this is mysticism mixed with asceticism. The social dimension is almost completely lacking, and criticism of the total social and cultural order with a view to the establishment of a full Christian order in the brotherhood and church of the living Christ in the midst of the present world is missing. This type of "following" Christ does not meet the fullness and richness of the New Testament concept and is not at all the Anabaptist idea. Thomas á Kempis and all those many who follow in his train evade the conflict with the world, avoid the constructive labor of establishing the true church, and thus escape the real cross-bearing experience of true discipleship. There is more kinship between Thomas and the later Pietists than the Anabaptists.

Another type of discipleship comes still closer to the Anabaptists; it is that of the so-called Spiritualists of the Reformation, including Schwenkfeld and possibly even Hans Denk. These men caught the vision of full discipleship but decided to delay the practice of it until a more convenient season. At least this was the case with Schwenkfeld. He was very close to the Anabaptists but advised his followers to refrain from openly organizing a church, evidently because of the opposition and danger of persecution. Hans Denk at the end of his life regretted that he had baptized and would have merely preached the new faith without implementing it in an organization had he lived. Even Melchior Hofmann, when the going got hot, called for an armistice of two years with no baptizing. All these men shrank from the ultimate price of open discipleship in the crucial moment.

Now it is of the essence of discipleship in the Anabaptist concept that one openly takes his stand for his Lord regardless of consequences. There was to be no cryptodiscipleship. Did not Jesus himself say, "If you are ashamed of me, I shall be ashamed of you in that day"? What the Anabaptist accepted as truth, that he put into practice in life forthwith. He came to grips directly with the world which is an enemy to God. It is this quality of what we moderns call "existentialism" which was deeply characteristic of the Anabaptist theology of discipleship, the inseparability of belief and practice, faith and life. To profess the new birth meant a new life. To take the name of Christ meant to take his spirit and his nature. To promise obedience to him meant actually to live out and carry through his principles and do his works. To claim the cleansing and redemption from sin which baptism symbolized, meant to leave off the sins and lusts of the flesh and the spirit and to live a holy life. To take up the cross daily meant to go out into conflict with the world of sin and evil and fight the good fight of faith, taking gladly the blows and buffetings of the world. To be a disciple meant to teach and to observe all things whatsoever the Master had taught and commanded.

This absolute discipleship applied to all areas of life. It meant a church composed only of disciples, not a mixture of disciples and worldlings. It meant that brethren in need should share their material goods. It meant a Christianizing of all social relationships, a substituting of the simplicity and sincerity of Christ for the pride and vanity of the world. It meant rejection of violence and bloodshed and warfare. It meant far more than the Brethren of that day realized or were able to work out in theoretical programs and statements. But it was even so with the Master and his earliest disciples, the apostles, who proclaimed and exemplified great principles of life without developing systematic and programmatic formulae for their application. Slavery, for instance, was not specifically condemned and forbidden by either Jesus or Paul, nor even warfare as such; but the life and love which they brought and taught inevitably mean the elimination of slavery and warfare. Implicit in the basic Anabaptist theology of discipleship was a new order which was bound to come as the discipleship was practiced.

I am aware that the thesis which I have proposed of the centrality and regulative character of the Anabaptist concept of discipleship requires the fullest possible documentation if it is to be accepted, and I hope to deliver this documentation in time. It is not available for this presentation today. However, all of us recall such striking phrases as that of Hans Denk, *"Niemand vermag Christum wahrlich zu erkennen, es sei denn, dass er ihm nachfolge im Leben,"* and the complaints of the Swiss Brethren and Menno Simons that the preaching of the preachers of the state churches failed to produce "fruit," that faith to be living must be "in evidence," etc. So, I rest my case at this point with its simple assertion and commend it to you for the most careful scrutiny and entreat analysis. I hold it to be the true Christian way, the gospel.

4.1

Anabaptist Studies 1[1]

The Anabaptist Dissent: Swiss Origins and Issues

WILLIAM KLASSEN

Introduction

Several major turning points in the history of the church can be pinpointed. One of these is without question the declaration by Constantine in the early fourth century that Christianity would no longer be persecuted, nor merely tolerated, but actually promoted as the official state religion of the Roman Empire. This was such a radical about-face that it took decades to get acclimatized to the change. Whether it was a curse or a blessing is still debated.

An equally profound change in the history of the church took place in the sixteenth century. The dramatic story of Martin Luther's life has been told in a scintillating way by Roland Bainton in his book *Here I Stand* and does not need to be retold here. The importance of the Reformation is taken for granted; above all it should be expressly stated that the Anabaptists are considered legitimate children of the Reformation. Their enemies called them "deformers" or others more kind "stepchildren" of the Reformation.

---

1. The first of five lectures published here, originally presented to a Student Services Summer Seminar, Elkhart, Ind., August, 1964.

Most writers in the field of history have at least until 1900 found it convenient to ignore them; and Adolph Harnack spoke for many scholars when he stated that Anabaptists do not belong in any treatment of history of Christian doctrine. It should be recalled that he said so because they did not have any *specifically* distinctive doctrines. In the field of ethics Harnack admitted that it was quite a different story. So Harnack's statement itself argues for seeing the Anabaptists as organic members of the Reformation.

But why do we spend so much time and pay so much attention to this one group of Christians? For us, whose spiritual and cultural heritage goes back 400 years, it is impossible to consign the witness of these men to the unilluminated caves of history nor can we allow their testimonies to repose dormant in our excellent historical libraries.

Scholars of various fields and disciplines have capitalized on the new sources available since 1900 for Anabaptist study. While many of these have taken a more or less academic interest, others have allowed these sources to speak with unparalleled vigor to the problems that confront us in our own day. Historians of the future will certainly point to the Anabaptist Renaissance in our brotherhood as one of the most significant events of the twentieth century. On this renaissance we have built such programs as Mennonite interdenominational cooperation, our peace witness, our mutual aid programs, etc. The flourishing of our institutions of higher learning, mission work, and hospitals, while not directly instigated by the recovery of the Anabaptist vision, still to a large extent developed simultaneously and these activities were mutually stimulating.

Yet the major reason for the study of Anabaptist-Mennonite beliefs is to test their conception of what it means to do the will of God. To what extent did this group of devout followers of Jesus Christ bequeath a legacy to us which deserves not only serious study, but also a measure of emulation? Where does our understanding of the word of God differ from theirs? Ultimately, we are driven back to the lordship of Christ as expressed today in his community, the church, applying itself to all problems, basing itself upon all sorts of authority available, including the Scriptures. For this reason, considerable time will be spent looking not only at Anabaptist-Mennonite beliefs, but also at specific New Testament texts which were so determinative for the early Anabaptists. It is impossible to reconstruct the early history of the Anabaptist movement completely and to find all the reasons that led to the formulation of their position. Nevertheless, we can recapture something of the dynamic mood and the vibrant enthusiasm of those Christians. For the purpose of our discussion we find it convenient to follow the outline of Fritz Blanke in his book *Brothers in Christ*. At some points it will be corrected by the later and more thorough research of John Howard Yoder.

The beginnings of Anabaptism can be located at Zurich, Switzerland, and dated January 1525. Fritz Blanke has ingeniously divided the early story into five acts.

Act 1: The Beginning of Alienation

While connections with Luther were not deep or intimate, the connections of the Anabaptists with Ulrich Zwingli were extensive. Zwingli was the leader of the Swiss Reformation, especially in the city of Zurich. By council decree, Zurich became Protestant in January 1523. The fact that the council so decreed does not mean, however, that it was a popular majority decision. In fact, Zwingli himself tells us that there were three classes:

1. The negative Protestants who merely opposed Catholicism. Their only faith was "we are no longer Catholics nor care to be."

2. The Libertinist Protestants who saw in the gospel a license to do as they desired.

3. The third group were those who "worked in the Word of God," i.e. they were evangelical pastors of Zurich who were surrounded by their friends and followers.

To this latter group belonged two of Zwingli's closest associates: Conrad Grebel and Felix Manz. Grebel was the son of a city councilor while Manz was the son of a choir director. Both had become Protestant through Zwingli who had preached the New Testament with singular power ever since 1519. As early as August 1522, Zwingli gave evidence of his respect and appreciation for Grebel by closing one of his earliest writings with one of Grebel's poems.

The first evidence of disagreement between Zwingli and Grebel appears in the fall of 1523. In October, the council had called a meeting to ascertain what attitude should be taken toward the Catholic mass and icons, especially to see whether the Bible threw any light on this problem. On the basis of this discussion the council desired eventually to take some action, either retaining or removing both the mass and icons. On the evening of

October 27, the discussion about the mass was completed with the conclusion that the Roman teaching, according to which the mass is the repetition of a sacrifice of Christ, was false. Having reached this conclusion the council prepared to move on to a new theme when Conrad Grebel asked for the floor and requested that the council at this very meeting, while they were still gathered there, give some leadership and direction on how the practical administration of the Lord's Supper was to take place in the future. Zwingli replied that the how and when of such a decision must be left with the chief councilors. He opposed immediate action because (1) the council had not promised such and (2) he himself had basic reservations against making an immediate change. The people after all are not ready for liturgical changes, first they must be more thoroughly instructed in the word of God.

It must be observed that both Conrad Grebel and Zwingli had the same goal, namely, the total removal of the abuses introduced by Catholicism. The difference was that Grebel wanted them removed at one blow, while Zwingli felt that by preaching decisively and consistently against the abuses and by positive proclamation of the gospel, the abuses would gradually die off. Grebel here takes the stance of the radical reformer who seeks immediate action while Zwingli is the conservative calling for restraint. The key word in Zwingli's program is "*Schonung*" (caution) to protect the weaker brethren. We may ask which is the right approach, but the answer to that question is not simple. We cannot always say which solution is correct in history. Those who would argue that a church group caught in a transition of language ought to take immediate steps, do not take into consideration the great emotional and psychological factors which accompany all change. Such factors certainly were also at work in the change over which Zwingli and Grebel disagreed.

There were in addition character differences between Grebel and Zwingli which contributed greatly to the different postures adopted. Some have said that the difference lies in the fact that Grebel was legalistic while Zwingli was not. This has been disputed and with good reason by John Howard Yoder who concluded that they agreed in everything, the only difference being that Zwingli was willing to wait with the institution of changes until the people had agreed to them, while Grebel wanted to institute these changes forthwith.[2] One might also raise the question of the nature of leadership. According to Grebel the people respond to courageous leadership

---

2. Yoder, *Die Gespräche zwischen Täufern*, 25.

but according to Zwingli one must prepare the people for these changes and assume that the word will have its effect in due time.

At this time cordiality still existed between these two men, yet the letters of Grebel to his brother-in-law Vadian show increasing impatience. On December 18, 1523, he wrote that at the second disputation the leading theologians of Zurich had "made the Word of God stand on its head, trampled it underfoot, and taken it into slavery."[3] The reasons that he gives for this are that the mass is still for the most part being celebrated as usual, in Latin, that the congregation was not permitted to drink wine, and that certain baptismal abuses still existed. Indeed, until Easter 1525, Zwingli and his associates baptized infants according to Catholic usage, including exorcism, breathing upon them, touching them with spittle, and anointing them with oil.

Act II: A Plan that Failed

Because Grebel could not tolerate this slow process of change he and Manz proposed to Zwingli that he issue a call that all who would follow Christ should come over to his side. They were convinced that the Zurich people would follow this call in droves and that a Christian majority then could elect a new Christian council. It was their hope and their assumption that Zwingli would still carry the main leadership in this movement. In this proposal there is no mention of a new baptism or of the believers as a minority or that Christians could not be members of the council. Grebel and Manz are still looking for a blueprint for the new church, but it has not yet been found. Since this plan failed because Zwingli would not respond to it, Grebel and Manz had to rethink their strategy.

The result of this reappraisal is seen in a long letter written by Grebel for his friends to Thomas Müntzer (September 5, 1524) in Saxony.[4]

Act III: The New Program

The letter written to Müntzer contains the outlines of the new program on which Grebel and Manz now seek to embark. It contains the criticism that Zwingli still tolerates the Catholic ceremonies of baptism and the Lord's

---

3. Blanke, *Brothers in Christ*, 10.
4. Williams and Mergal, *Spiritual and Anabaptist*, 73–83.

Supper. Grebel complains that the solution that has been idolized in Zurich is to go slowly and to be cautious in changing the Catholic rites.[5] It is apparent that this letter to Müntzer represents a drastic change from the previous approach. For one thing the church is now no longer seen as a popular movement but as a minority group of those people who believe and live correctly. The church of Zwingli is rejected now because it is every man's church, because in it external faith and compromise rule the day. John Yoder has correctly seen that the most striking feature about this letter is "the totally new concept of the church and the new self-understanding which is expressed herein."[6] The three points which are most salient in the document are the concern for believer's baptism, an insistence on a separation of the church from both the support of and control by the state, and a programmatic renunciation of war.[7]

The reform program which is now spelled out by Grebel and Manz includes the observance of baptism and the Lord's Supper according to apostolic manner. As this is done, every resemblance to the Roman Catholic mass is to be removed. Instead the Lord's Supper is to be a simple evening meal, with the use of the words of institution practiced not in a church building but in the homes of the believers, without monks' garb, using ordinary bread and utensils as a symbolic eating which portrays the fellowship of Christians among each other and with Christ. Baptism is to be confined only to believers.

As Blanke has observed, "these are indications of a concept of the church found nowhere else at that time." Where did it come from? Grebel himself says, "We listened to Zwingli's sermons and his writings, but one day we took the Bible itself and were better instructed." What Grebel means by this is that after they had read the Scripture independently, they went beyond Zwingli on a number of points. Several times Grebel states, "We act only according to the Word but Zwingli does not."

This emerges as a particularly striking point when we remember that Zwingli considered it the main virtue of his church that it had been built solely upon the word of God. Thus, both Grebel and Zwingli claim to base all of their actions on the word. Perhaps we have here two differing conceptions of the Scriptures. According to Zwingli Christ alone is binding, justification by faith alone applies, wherever Scripture addresses itself to the

---

5. Williams and Mergal, *Spiritual and Anabaptist*, 77.

6. Yoder, *Die Gespräche zwischen Täufern*, 31.

7. Williams and Mergal, *Spiritual and Anabaptist*, 72.

question of the external order of the church and whatever it may have to say on the subject, is not binding. In no sense is the church today bound by the externals of church order practiced in the New Testament age.

For Grebel and his group such a distinction between outer form and inner essence simply does not exist. The above quote from Grebel already seems to point in the direction of a stricter biblicism than that which we encounter in Zwingli. This seems to appear also in Grebel's attitude toward the singing which accompanies the mass. In his letter to Müntzer he says, "and do thou drop singing at the mass, and act in all things only according to the Word, bring forth and establish by the word the usages of the apostles."[8] At another point, speaking on the issue of singing he says:

> We understand that thou hast translated the mass into German and hast introduced new German hymns. That cannot be for the good, since we find nothing taught in the New Testament about singing, no example of it. Paul scolds the learned among the Corinthians more than he praises them because they mumbled in meeting as if they sang, just as the Jews and the Italians chant their words in song fashion. Since singing in Latin grew up without divine instruction and apostolic example and custom without producing good or edifying, it will still less edify in German and will create a faith of outward appearance only. Paul very clearly forbids singing in Eph 5:19 and Col 3:16 since he says and teaches that they are to speak to one another and teach one another with psalms and spiritual songs, and if anyone would sing, he should sing and give thanks in his heart. Whatever we are not taught by clear passages or examples must be regarded as forbidden, just as if it were written: "this do not; sing not." Christ in the Old and especially in the New Testament bids his messengers simply proclaim the Word. Paul, too, says that the word of Christ profits us, not the song. Whoever sings poorly gets vexation by it; whoever can sing well gets conceit. We must not follow our notions, we must add nothing to the word and take nothing from it.[9]

It is in this letter that Grebel first expresses the ideal of voluntary church membership which lies at the heart of the free church movement. In the same letter Grebel, however, recommends not only withdrawal from the mass church, but also from certain political responsibilities. To Müntzer he says, a truly believing Christian can neither accept a governmental

---

8. Williams and Mergal, *Spiritual and Anabaptist*, 77.
9. Williams and Mergal, *Spiritual and Anabaptist*, 75–76.

office nor participate in war. The Christian's lot is to suffer. Every revolution, every self-defense by means of force, every use of the sword is denied the Christian. This is September 1524. The group around Grebel probably numbered around twenty. With the manifesto drawn up a period of prayerful waiting ensues.

Act IV: Final Attempts at Reconciliation

The fourth act consists of some final attempts at reconciliation. The issue of baptism came to the fore because there was an increasing number of men who hesitated to have their children baptized. During the time from October to December 1524, two Tuesday discussions were held on this issue at the request of Grebel. These were not public and did not accomplish much. Manz addressed himself to the council directly with a writing entitled, *The Protest*. Zwingli also drew up a writing in December 1524, in which he detailed seven groups of people that were stirring up unrest among the population. Among these he did not consider the Anabaptists as most dangerous but considered them merely a religious group. The tensions with them were not of a material nature. He begs Grebel to stress the essentials of the faith and put aside all pride and not to stress the externals.

Act V: The Break

The fifth and final act culminated in the break between Zwingli and the Grebel group. The council had called for a public disputation on January 17, 1525. In actual fact there was no disputation at all because already those who denied the validity of infant baptism were considered deviants. The council decided on January 18, 1525, that henceforth all children must be baptized within eight days after birth. If not, the parents were to be banned. On the 21st of January, all public gatherings of those who opposed infant baptism were banned and Grebel and Manz were denied the privilege of public speech. Four others were banished, apparently because the council felt that its traditional security was being threatened. Increasingly the brethren saw this as God's hour. On the evening of January 21, 1525, they gathered in the house of Felix Manz in Zurich. After a period of prayer together Jörg Blaurock asked Grebel to baptize him which Grebel did and then Jörg in return baptized all the rest. Here Anabaptism began. Other baptisms followed but the decisive act had taken place.

In the practice of these rites we note an apostolic simplicity which also characterized the observance of the Lord's Supper. Both are defined as acts of commitment of love toward God and commitment to lead a new life in God and as a token of brotherly love for each other. The nature of these assemblies is probably closest to small group revival meetings. At one point at least we hear that Hans Bruggbach was moved during the meeting to make confession and receive baptism. Ruedi Thomann described one of the meetings as consisting of Bible discussion, evangelism, and the Lord's Supper.

The radical break represented here with tradition can be well illustrated by the reaction of some of the people involved in these meetings. For example, H. Thomann tells us that the evening when he saw the lay people participating in baptism and the Lord's Supper he perspired from fear. One can well imagine the emotions of this old man who had been taught to respect the dignity of the Lord's Supper and baptism and the importance of the priestly role as he saw all of these being ignored. On another occasion the same man, when he saw three being baptized, said "my hair stood on end," or "my hair took to the hills." We see in the whole movement a radical questioning of the past and the traditional. Perhaps most dramatically this is expressed in the actions of Blaurock, who on January 29, 1525, being stirred as he saw his pastor going up to the pulpit, cried, "Not you, but I am sent to preach!" When his regular pastor finally got to preaching Blaurock repeatedly interrupted him until the pastor finally decided to quit, but the congregation would not hear of it. As he went up again to the pulpit and asked the people to bring their concerns to him in person, Blaurock felt struck by this rebuke and called out the words, "My house shall be called a house of prayer, but you have made it a den of thieves." The demonstration did not convince anyone as being peaceful, especially since Blaurock had a whip with him which he flailed against the bench. Finally, he was evicted by a city official. Some eight months later at Hinwil on the fifteenth of October 1525, Blaurock began to preach while the congregation was waiting for its regular pastor. Among other things he said, "Whose place is this? If it is God's place where His Word is to be proclaimed, then I am here as one commissioned by the Father to proclaim the Word of God." More is involved here than merely the actions of some misguided hotheads. Clearly Blaurock and many others were driven by a deep consciousness of calling (*Sendungsbewusstsein*) which led them to usurp the pulpit.

Yet the challenge to the order of the community was too great to tolerate. The city invoked the old Justinian Code which allowed them to ban and to punish by death anyone who disrupted the order of the community. Conrad Grebel was spared this kind of punishment because he died of the plague in August 1526. Manz was drowned after his sentence on January 5, 1527. The charge against him was

> because contrary to Christian order and custom he had become involved in Anabaptism, . . . because he confessed having said that he wanted to gather those who wanted to accept Christ and follow Him, and unite himself with them through baptism . . . so that he and his followers separated themselves from the Christian church and were about to raise up and prepare a sect of their own, . . . because he had condemned capital punishment, . . . since such doctrine is harmful to the unified usage of all Christendom, and leads to offense, insurrection, and sedition against the government . . . Manz shall be delivered to the executioner, who shall tie his hands, put him into a boat, take him to the lower hut, there strip his bound hands over his knees, place a stick between his knees and arms, and thus push him into the water and let him perish in the water; thereby he shall have atoned to the law and justice. . . . His property shall also be confiscated by my lords.[10]

With the death of Grebel and the execution of Manz only Blaurock was left but soon new leaders appeared to give leadership to the movement. One of the most outstanding of these leaders was Balthasar Hubmaier. He was undoubtedly the most learned of the early Anabaptist leaders. In spite of the fact that his position on government was not accepted by all Anabaptists, his teaching on baptism, the use of the ban, and other central Anabaptist beliefs continued to deeply influence the major Anabaptist thinkers. Hubmaier became an Anabaptist in 1525 at Eastertime. He traveled a great deal, but his major work was at Waldshut where his congregation became first of all reformed, then Anabaptist. In 1526 and 1527 he lived in the Moravian town of Nikolsburg where again his work was crowned with eminent success. He died in 1528 but his literary work continued to challenge both the Anabaptists and the larger Reformation.

In summary the issues raised by the early Anabaptists would appear to be the following:

---

10. Estep, *Anabaptist Story*, 30–31.

1. Can the church be free from the support and control of the state?
2. Can ecclesiastical practices be related to experience in such a way that the external rite and the inner experience are seen as one?
3. Can men entrust their personal destiny and the welfare of the group to radical obedience to God's word?
4. Can Christian love become a cohesive force in society or does community always imply external means of perpetuation and preservation?

Theses

1. Anabaptism had its origin within the Protestant Reformation and its earliest beginnings cannot be understood apart from that origin.
2. The growing need to go a separate way from that taken by Zwingli stemmed from Zwingli's failure to allow full and free discussion of the issues, his vacillation, and from the more radical courage to break with tradition displayed by Grebel and his friends.
3. The challenge to the clergy as demonstrated by Jörg Blaurock was so drastic that it constituted a major threat to the Zurich Constantinian synthesis.
4. At the heart of the Anabaptist movement was an intensive study of Scriptures, prayer, and a genuine revival of spiritual concerns.
5. The awareness of sins committed, the faith that in Christ these had been forgiven, and the conviction that it was possible to walk in the power of the resurrection under the lordship of Christ form the center of the religious beliefs of the early Swiss Brethren.

4.2

Anabaptist Studies 2

Advance and Consolidation: South Germany and the Vision Refocused

WILLIAM KLASSEN

If the cradle of Anabaptism is to be located in Switzerland it is clear that its major forward movement and its consolidation took place in South Germany. The connections between the early Swiss and the South Germans are so extensive that some have made a case for an independent origin in South Germany. Jan J. Kiwiet offered the suggestion that Denck and Hut began Anabaptism in South Germany independent of the Swiss Brethren. While this suggestion has not received widespread support, it is generally recognized that we have too long neglected the South German phase of the early movement. Thanks to some imaginative work by Kiwiet and the thorough research of Herb Klassen and Walter Klaassen our attention has been drawn to the Anabaptist centers of Augsburg and Strasbourg, and the leaders of the movement in these parts. It is tempting to imagine that Anabaptism here flourished independent of Swiss influence, but it is also fallacious. Differences in emphasis there were to be sure. At times there were even breaks in fellowship.

For the Swiss Brethren position the Schleitheim Confession represents the most important document to be found anywhere in Anabaptism.

Drafted on February 24, 1527, at Schleitheim on the border of the Swiss Confederacy, it represents the product of considerable discussion on seven major issues. It is a product of agreement and their position is defined over against the false brethren who are stressing the "freedom of the spirit and of Christ." They "have missed the truth and to their condemnation are given over to lasciviousness and self-indulgence of the flesh. They think faith and love may do and permit everything, and nothing will harm them nor condemn them since they are believers."[1] Who are these false brethren? Are they the Swiss radicals around St. Gall who were being carried away by their enthusiasm? Are they the South Germans? The Lutherans? Research will still need to be done on this subject. For the time being it may be noted that the presence of "false brethren" caused the Swiss Brethren to develop ways of dealing with the dissenter. Before any of the major Reformed parties had developed a church order the Anabaptists met and talked about the things they agreed on and those which divided them and they produced this statement which became the rallying point for Anabaptism in these critical years. It was not a creedal statement meant to enforce uniformity or conformity. It was a statement of convictions to which the Lord had led them and which they considered vital to their common life in Christ. Such topics as God, Christology, etc., do not appear since there is no disagreement in these areas with the traditional creeds. The seven topics that are discussed and their comparative length are:

    Baptism, one paragraph
    The Ban, one paragraph
    Lord's Supper, two paragraphs
    Separation from the World, five paragraphs
    Church Leadership, two paragraphs
    The Place of Temporal Power (sword, etc.) seven paragraphs
    The Oath, five paragraphs

While the length of the paragraphs varies somewhat, the subjects which most engage their attention are separation from the world and the use of the sword and the oath. They go to great lengths to describe the difference between swearing and calling God as witness and rule out every occasion for the possible use of an oath. Likewise, on the matter of the sword they are agreed that it is not to be used under any circumstances nor is the Christian to participate in the affairs of state because he has more important things to do. Christ's example also plays a major role here. The major

---

1. Fosdick, "Schleitheim Confession," 286–87.

reasons why it is not appropriate for a Christian to serve as a magistrate are: "The governmental magistracy is according to the flesh, but the Christian magistracy is according to the Spirit; their houses and dwelling remain in this world, but the Christian's citizenship is in heaven; the weapons of their conflict and war are carnal and against the flesh only, but the Christian's weapons are spiritual, against the fortification of the devil."[2]

The importance of Schleitheim cannot be overestimated. It is later cited as authoritative by a close co-worker of Marpeck, named Leopold Scharnschlager. It demonstrates that while the Anabaptists did not take their problems to the state for solution, they did have ways of coping with disagreements when they arose within the church. The question of church order thus became an important issue. They believed that there was an "order of the spirit" which allowed Christians to deal with sin in such a way that the community be strengthened, and the individual redeemed from it.

The leader of the community which brought the Schleitheim Confession into being was Michael Sattler. He is also the bridge personality between South Germany and Switzerland in the years 1526–27. He had gone to Strasbourg in the beginning of 1526 where Capito received him into his home. He left there after having met Hans Denck and Ludwig Hätzer to go to Horb where he worked until January 1527. He was executed on May 20, 1527. Moving descriptions of his martyrdom have been preserved and published in English translation by Williams in his volume, *Spiritual and Anabaptist Writers*.[3] One of the interesting charges against him was that he had taught that if the Turks would come we should not resist them. To this he answers:

> It is written: Thou shalt not kill. We must not defend ourselves against the Turks and others of our persecutors, but are to beseech God with earnest prayer to repel and resist them. But that I said that if, warring *were* right, I would rather take the field against so-called Christians who persecute, capture, and kill pious Christians than against the Turks for the following reason. The Turk is a true Turk, knows nothing of the Christian faith, and is a Turk after the flesh. But you who would be Christians and who make your boast of Christ persecute the pious witnesses of Christ and are Turks after the spirit![4]

2. Fosdick, "Schleitheim Confession," 292.
3. Williams and Mergal, *Spiritual and Anabaptist*, 138–44.
4. Williams and Mergal, *Spiritual and Anabaptist*, 141.

The martyrdom of Sattler profoundly shook his friends in the larger Reformation at Strasbourg. They saw his depth of devotion and they also saw the extent to which the authorities would go to crush the Anabaptist movement. Not only did they reject such a drastic manner of dealing with Anabaptists, they were convinced that some Anabaptists could be reasoned into departing from their Anabaptist faith.

Strasbourg had formed the hub of Anabaptist activity in South Germany. It was a haven of Anabaptists because of its widely lauded religious liberty. The Reformed leadership, Bucer and Capito, sought a lenient policy, in part because temperamentally they were suited only to that kind of policy, and partly because they felt it religiously and politically unwise to deal with dissenters in such a way. Thus, we have the remarkable record that at Strasbourg only one Anabaptist was ever punished by death and the charge against him was immorality. South Germany as a whole was blessed with an array of influential leaders who either lived there or directly influenced South Germany with their writings. These men did more to positively define the mission of Anabaptism than any one other group. If the painful break was made by the Swiss, it is clear that the South Germans gave the positive forward thrust to the movement. If the Swiss looked back to the New Testament Church and sought to restore it in its pristine purity, the South German Anabaptists looked forward and worked for the day when they would contribute to the windup of history by their faithfulness to the mission with which the Lord had entrusted them.

Hans Denck

Among the early South German leaders Hans Denck stands out as an intellectually brilliant and extremely sensitive person. He was probably born around 1500 and died in 1527. He was a humanist and a scholar, having served as teacher and as rector at a school in Nürenburg. He also worked for a while as a printer-corrector. As a writer he was very intellectual, dealing a good deal with doctrinal issues such as the love of God. He was baptized in May of 1526 by Hubmaier in Augsburg. In November 1526, he arrived in Strasbourg but had to leave by Christmas of that year. On April 13, 1527, he along with Ludwig Hätzer brought out the first edition of the prophets translated directly from the Hebrew original.

Denck had a sophisticated mind which was able to detect paradoxes and difficulties within Scripture. He wrestled for the correct interpretation of Scripture and sought to harmonize those parts which seemed to contradict each other. There is no doubt that through his knowledge of Hebrew and his translation work in the prophets he made a significant contribution to the history of the German Bible. Luther used him, not as much as some Mennonite scholars have assumed, but more than some Lutheran scholars are willing to admit. Luther himself made no secret of the fact that he had used Denck's translation and we should not worry too much if he did so without dropping a footnote.

What the legacy of Denck for Anabaptism was is indeed hard to say. Part of the interpretation of Denck's life has been plagued by an uncritical acceptance of a book or writing attributed to him which is a so-called recantation of his position. It is possible that he signed a statement toward the end of his life when he was sick, recanting in part his position. On the other hand, Denck's attachment to the institutional church and the order seen so clearly in the Schleitheim confession was always shallow. He baptized only one person, although indeed a very significant one, namely, Hans Hut. If his writings were to be trusted, he deviated from the Schleitheim position on the oath. The charge of universalism, meaning that even the devil eventually will he saved, has been leveled at Denck for four centuries, but no evidence exists in his writing that he actually taught this even though *The Mennonite Encyclopedia* attributes this view to him. What appears to be clear is that he stressed very much the love of God and thus laid himself open to the charge of teaching universalism.

Hans Hut

If Hans Denck was the intellectual leader of South Germany, and it is evident that his writings exerted a profound influence on South German Anabaptism, it is clear that Hans Hut was a devout and avid missionary in the movement. The Great Commission was the driving edge of all that he did. He was a book binder and seller by trade and his work caused him to be a frequent visitor at Wittenberg. A poster issued by the council of Nürenberg on March 26, 1527, describes him as follows: "The highest and chiefest leader of the Anabaptists is John Hut, a well-educated, clever fellow, rather tall, a peasant with light brown cropped hair and a blonde mustache. He is dressed in a grey, sometimes a black riding coat, a broad grey hat, and grey pants."

Hut had close connections with the radical Thomas Müntzer from whom he likely derived his eschatological interest. He had some narrow escapes during the Peasants' War. In 1525 he was at Frankenhausen when the war broke out and the thought of the imminent coming of Christ kindled in him a sort of enthusiasm for this war. When on the next day the peasants marched to battle, he at first went up the hill with them, but "because the fighting was too thick" he hastened back to Frankenhausen.

He was baptized on May 26, 1526, by Hans Denck. His preaching centered around the Great Commission. He tells us himself that he always began with the Great Commission and the text "to preach the gospel to every creature." He also preached judgment and the imminent end of the world. The center of his proclamation, however, was the lordship of Christ here and now. On the theme of baptism he distinguished between three kinds of baptism: (1) baptism by the spirit which signifies the covenant that God made with us; (2) baptism by water, which is a commitment on our part to the community of grace, and is a sign of our obedience to the lordship of Christ; (3) baptism by blood, which signifies martyrdom and paying the supreme price for serving Christ. He believed that these three baptisms are, in fact, one, and their witness is required on earth (1 John 5:6–8).

Hut and Hubmaier met at Nicolsburg where the Turkish question was vigorously discussed. It is not clear, however, exactly what position Hut took on such issues as the sword. The famous "Martyrs' Synod" held August 20, 1527, at which more than sixty Anabaptist leaders convened, gave a prominent place to two concerns which appeared strongly in Hut's thinking. Its major purpose was to appoint missionaries or messengers to go out in all directions two by two. Another major item on the agenda was to discuss the theological issue of eschatology. On this matter there was a division between those who set the date of the return of Christ in the spring of 1528 and those who cautioned against any such specific details. At this synod it was agreed to discontinue the details of eschatological preaching and Hut especially was prevailed upon to discontinue such specifics, yet he continued to believe that Christ would return in 1528.

It must be noted that on an issue on which there was disagreement the method pursued by the South Germans was the same as that of Schleitheim. They had what is at one place called a concilium, which may mean that they had several meetings in an attempt to iron out their difficulties. For South German Anabaptism it was a most significant meeting. It came seven months after the meeting at Schleitheim.

Since Hut was a prominent leader among the Anabaptists and a most effective missionary the authorities soon attempted to imprison him. He was first seized and tried on September 16, 1527. Fortunately, his court records have been preserved and we receive a great deal of information from these records about his life. In fact, these are the major sources which provide some glimpses into his life and teaching.

Two reports of his death are preserved. According to one he tried to escape by igniting some straw. The other is given by his son when he says, "Hut was racked in the tower and then released. He lay like one dead. They went away leaving a candle in the cell which ignited the straw. When they returned he was dead." The officials took the dead body to court on a chair, tied the chair to the executioner's cart, sentenced it to die and burnt it at the stake on December 7, 1527.

Hut's importance for the movement consists in the fact that he was well educated and clever. He was a most forceful leader of early Anabaptists and although only four brief writings and some hymns have been preserved it is clear that he exerted a profound influence on the total movement including the Moravian branch of Anabaptism.

Taking both of these men together we would have to observe that under their leadership Anabaptism joined the scholarly concern, the involvement in Bible translation and theological issues with a great missionary thrust. For some of the Anabaptists the fact that Columbus had discovered a new world a scant generation earlier presented the greatest challenge for the gospel. While other reformers argued that the Great Commission applied only to the apostles and their generation, Hut and men like him bent all their energies to the proclamation of the gospel wherever people lived. A new world lay beckoning before them. They were called to proclaim the gospel to this world, and nothing could deter them from this great task. While Denck has often been considered on the fringes of Anabaptism, there is no doubt that as an intellectual leader he stands among the front rank of Anabaptists. Because of his scholarly involvement he seems to have had only slight interest in the church and its organizational forms. Whatever may be the explanation of some of Denck's actions, it may not be too much to see in his relationship to Hans Hut a rather significant joining together of two types, the missionary evangelical type and the scholarly type. Both are needed in the church and both surely can exist side by side.

Moravia

The Anabaptists moved not only toward South Germany but increasingly toward Moravia and the largest group which settled here was the Hutterian brethren. By 1535 they had received vigorous leadership from men totally committed to the practice of communism because this is the way they felt the church in Jerusalem had lived. The Hutterian brethren were also deeply committed to a missionary program with their messengers going out to all parts of Europe.

A number of Anabaptist leaders taught something closely approximating the Hutterian point of view but stopping short of an implementation of a communistic way of life. Ambrosius Spittlemaier said, for example:

> Nobody can inherit the kingdom unless he is poor with Christ, for a Christian has nothing of his own; no place where he can lay his head. A real Christian should not even have enough property on earth to be able to stand on it with one foot. This does not mean that he should go and lie down in the woods and not have a trade, or that he should not have fields and meadows, or that he should not work, but only that he might not think they are for his own use and be tempted to say: this house is mine, this field is mine, this dollar is mine. Rather he should say it is ours, even as we pray, our Father. In summary, a Christian should not have anything of his own but should have all things in common with his brother, i.e., not allow him to suffer need. In other words, I will not work that my house be filled, that my larder be supplied with meat, but rather I will see that my brother has enough, for a Christian looks more to his neighbor than to himself. Whoever desires to be rich in this world, who is concerned that he miss nothing when it comes to his person and property, who is honored by men and feared by them, who refuses to prostrate himself at the feet of the Lord ... will be humbled.[5]

For Spittlemaier this did not mean that the Christian could not own any property, as is clear. He was not a Hutterian, but he believed that for all practical purposes we belong to each other and that our property is not privately owned. It is clear that the Hutterians did not follow him in the external application of this point of view.

---

5. Klassen, "Ambrosius Spittlemaier," 600.

Summary

What would appear from our look at the second phase of Anabaptism is that in South Germany and Moravia progress was made toward the ordering of the external community, yet the main thing that stayed Anabaptism was its high conception of the apostolate and its continuing deep commitment to the word of God. Hut the missionary, Denck the scholar, but above all the costly martyrdoms of Spittlemaier, Schlaffer, and Schiemer continued to strengthen the Anabaptists in their cause even as their leaders fell by the sword.

Theses

1. Anabaptism after 1527 can best be understood as the first vigorous missionary movement.
2. In the sacramental controversies of 1530 the Anabaptists suggest a third alternative which saw sacraments as living realities.
3. The Old Testament must be seen as a pointer to the New and interpreted in the light of its fulfillment in Christ.
4. Man is justified by faith alone, but a living faith brings about visible signs of corporate renewal.
5. Man is accountable to God and his fellow Christians alone for actions in the realm of faith and not to the state.

4.3

Anabaptist Studies 3

Pilgram Marpeck: Covenant Community

WILLIAM KLASSEN

Wherever social revolutions take place the controls of human behavior tend to give way. The impact of the revolution is always an unknown factor. The Peasants' Revolt is a good example of this in the Reformation. The challenge that Anabaptism faced was the formation of a community which had certain built-in controls. In order to meet this challenge Anabaptism had to devise ways of purging its radicals or perhaps taming them, as well as making membership requirements so specific and clear that only those deeply committed to its essence would join it.

The multiplicity of portraits of Anabaptism as early as 1530 is clearly seen in Sebastian Franck's *Chronica*.[1] He lists a variety of deviants and Anabaptists known to him. The place where this issue was most directly faced was Strasbourg. The man who contributed most to the solution of this problem was Pilgram Marpeck. In order to more fully appreciate his contribution, it may be well to review the salient aspects of his life.

1. Franck, *Chronica, Zeitbuch und Geschichtsbibel*.

I. The Early Life of Marpeck (1500–1528)

The life of Pilgram Marpeck falls into four major periods. He was born and lived the first thirty years of his life in Rattenberg, Tyrol. He was a member of a prominent family and was himself appointed to the city council on June 11, 1525. On April 20 of the same year he was appointed a mining inspector which apparently provided him with a great deal of opportunity to meet miners directly. We have some indications that in the fall of 1527 the authorities asked him to collaborate with them in indicating to them who the members of the Anabaptist sect were, but he demurred at this request, apparently feeling that his contract did not call for this kind of work. It seemed to him to be an unnecessary confusion of the role of government and religious faith. Whatever was his exact religious alignment at this time, it is evident that by January 1528, he had to relinquish his position because of his religious convictions. His two houses were confiscated, and it was only later that his daughter and three adopted children received part of the money for these properties. The influences that were at work in Tyrol were mainly Anabaptist. Lutherans, while they had been active in the area, had not established a firm foothold, and it is possible that Marpeck, although he knew Lutheranism well, never himself became a Lutheran but changed directly from Roman Catholicism to Anabaptism. The influences of Hut, Schlaffer, and Schiemer were evident in the vicinity of Rattenberg, Marpeck's early home.

II. Strasbourg (1528–1532)

The second phase of Marpeck's life extends from 1528 to 1532 and can be designated the Strasbourg years. By September 19, 1528, he was enrolled as a citizen of the city; he worked for a salary in a city forest, being responsible for the water system of the city as well as firewood which was cut on the mountainside during the winter and then floated down the rivers in springtime.

In these crucial years Marpeck took a vigorous leadership role among the Anabaptists. Wilhelm Reublin had given good leadership to the church but now was no longer in the city. At the same time various other people with Anabaptist leanings had come to the city and had not helped to stabilize the group. There was, for example, John Bünderlin, who was a radical spiritualist having no use for the organized church or the Old or New

Testament but sought only to be guided by God's own Spirit. From 1529 to 1530 he wrote four books, three of which were published in Strasbourg and several of which were read among the Anabaptist meetings while Marpeck was in town. Bünderlin's radical rejection of all external ceremonies in the church, his rejection even of the written word of God, constituted a grave threat to the Anabaptists especially since Denck's own leadership would have made them receptive to this kind of approach. Sebastian Franck, also respected by the Anabaptists, moved very strongly in this direction.

Alongside of these more radical spiritualists we find a man like Schwenckfeld, who was a devout student of the Bible but to whom the external ceremonies of the church, discipline, and church organization were not too significant. Marpeck saw immediately that to follow this road would mean the dissolution of the Anabaptist church and cause it to dwindle into a conventicle. He wrote, therefore, two booklets in 1531 which addressed themselves to Bünderlin and Schwenckfeld and tried to counteract their influence among the Anabaptists. These books were discovered by the censors and then condemned because he advocated adult baptism in them, and even though his name was never attached to them they were attributed to him by the censors and have only recently been called to the attention of the scholarly world.

In addition to the spiritualists the radical eschatological emphasis of Hans Hut continued on in several prophets including Melchior Hofmann. Hofmann attracted a good deal of attention to himself in Strasbourg by his eschatological predictions, his vivid way of interpreting the book of Revelation for his contemporaries, and above all his insistence that he be imprisoned repeatedly. He eventually died in prison but for a while quite a few people followed his leadership.

As if these threats from within the movement were not serious enough, Anabaptism constantly had to defend itself alongside the wider Reformation. This was especially important in Strasbourg because of the competent leadership given to the Reformed cause by men like Bucer and others. Their sweet reasonableness provided the Anabaptists the only opportunity for extensive dialogue even though they were often evicted from the city. Marpeck found himself in an unusual position. For one thing he had acquired the respect of both Martin Bucer and Capito, and other city fathers, through his skillful work as an engineer. On the other hand, his enthusiasm and commitment to Anabaptism had not abated, and he continued to work vigorously for its strengthening. He continued to baptize and to proclaim the word and to give vigorous leadership to the Anabaptists during the four years he spent in Strasbourg. Attempts were made to draw up a church order, and the more Anabaptism moved toward a definable position, the closer scrutiny it received from the authorities. Because baptism of infants was falling off sharply the authorities felt something had to be done. In addition, no Anabaptist took the yearly vow to protect Strasbourg and this constituted a serious security threat to the city. Since Marpeck was a leader in all of this, it was logical that he himself be imprisoned, which actually took place in September 1531. He apparently did not stay in prison long on that occasion but by December 1531, he was imprisoned a second time. This time, since he refused to desist from his activities as Anabaptist leader, the case became considerably more serious.

Throughout December and most of January extensive discussions were carried on between Marpeck and the city council, in particular through its spokesman, Martin Bucer. We cannot visualize the situation unless we see the ministerial alliance and the city council as one voting body. These discussions at first were quite cordial and a serious attempt was made to bridge the gap between Bucer's position and that of Marpeck. Marpeck complained that the Old Testament was not receiving the proper attention in Bucer's reformation, he was concerned that the abomination of infant baptism was still being practiced and endorsed and above all that the gospel was being proclaimed under the banner of the state. If this was done the gospel was not really permitted freedom and therefore could not do its perfect work. As a result of these discussions Marpeck drew up his own confession of faith in January 1532, which has been published by John C. Wenger in 1938 in *The Mennonite Quarterly Review* and which gives us a fuller picture of his theological position than we have from the two booklets of 1531.[2] Although the council granted his request that he be permitted to stay until the fifteenth of January, to collect his back pay and also to dispose of his property, he had to leave by January 20, 1532, never to return. He refused to promise never to return because he said that he had no idea which way the Spirit of God would lead him and in the event that the Spirit would drive him to return to Strasbourg, his ultimate allegiance would have to be to the Spirit of God. Bucer took Marpeck seriously enough to write a detailed refutation of his confession of faith which fortunately also has been preserved.

---

2. Marpeck, "Pilgram Marpeck's Confession."

III. The Years in Switzerland and Moravia (1532–1544)

The third period of Marpeck's life was spent in Switzerland and Moravia. We have very few definite traces of the exact places where Marpeck worked. There is evidence that from 1535 following, he was at St. Gall, Switzerland, and in 1541 he appears among the Hutterites in Moravia. While he did not work for any length of time in Strasbourg, he did attempt both in Switzerland and in Moravia to unite the badly splintered Anabaptist movement into a unified whole. Indeed, this was his major concern during these twelve years culminating in a confession which he published in 1542 which was designed to draw together the many diverse Anabaptist groups.

When he traveled to Moravia in 1541 his reception among the Hutterites was far from enthusiastic. As the *Chronica* reports it, Marpeck arrived with the great ambition of uniting all the Anabaptists, but they did not even permit him to speak. They had considerable experience with other outsiders who had attempted to bring the Hutterites into the Anabaptist orbit and had discovered whenever these men were given a sounding board a split developed within their ranks. So in this case Marpeck was not even permitted the opportunity to pray with them. This upset him so much that he stated publicly that he would rather join the Turks or the Catholics than to join their congregation. It is understandable that the relations between the Hutterites and Marpeck would develop in this way since he had always taken a firm position that community of goods should not be made a test of church membership. Since he had written publicly about this it is understandable that they did not consider him a great asset to their group. Furthermore, they resisted any attempt to unify all of the Anabaptists since they felt strongly that their own peculiar position was not only in harmony with New Testament teaching, but also greatly blessed of God.

Tensions developed from another area, namely, the Swiss Brethren. At least in the regions of St. Gall and Appenzell the Swiss Brethren continued to resist Marpeck's unifying work and refused even to carry on correspondence with him after his departure from that city. Marpeck complains that they are carrying on such a rigid church program that many of their leaders are under the ban, some of them even under the double ban; he is uneasy about their restrictions of clothing and of the type of work which Christians can do, but his major complaint is that they are not allowing the processes of Christian discussion to take their course. There is obviously no hope for the unity of the church, if brothers will not listen to what their fellow members of the church have to say.

The publication of the *Confessional Book* in 1542 brought a storm, however, not from within the Anabaptist movement but from the fringes, namely, the Schwenckfelder conventicle.[3] Since a number of people in South Germany were wavering between Anabaptism and Schwenckfeld, it is understandable that Schwenckfeld saw the Confessional booklet as being directed against him and therefore responded eagerly to a request of one of his followers to reply to it. It is doubtful that Marpeck actually had Schwenckfeld in mind when he wrote the *Confessional Book,* but he did not hesitate to carry on the debate with Schwenckfeld. There is in fact evidence that Marpeck had in mind primarily the militant Anabaptists who had been so tragically misled at Münster when he wrote the confession. He used all of a book written by Rothmann, adding about a third of the manuscript in which he sought to correct the excesses and the delusions of Rothmann. He does so with acknowledgment that he is using other sources, but no one until recent times knew how extensive this "borrowing" was. The Rothmann book was in Westphalian dialect which Marpeck translated into South German. In this as in all of his works Marpeck worked very closely with Leopold Scharnschlager so that it is difficult to distinguish between Scharnschlager's and Marpeck's theology.

IV. Augsburg (1544–1556)

The fourth major period of Marpeck's life was spent in the city of Augsburg from 1544 to 1556. Augsburg had an active Anabaptist group from 1525 to 1530 but severe persecution almost extinguished the total movement there. However, political conditions had changed and by the early forties the climate was such that individual Anabaptists moved back to the city and made this the center of witness. Marpeck came as civil engineer and worked for twelve years in this capacity. Contemporary chroniclers praise him for his work even though in the religious realm he continued to get into trouble with the civil authorities. Repeated warnings, particularly toward the end of his life, were given and requests made that he desist from his religious activity, but his publishing and writing record is such that we can only judge that he ignored these requests. Indeed, the correspondence flowed freely from Augsburg to Moravia, to Strasbourg, to Switzerland,

---

3. Klassen, *Covenant and Community*, 45–46.

during these years and three major contributions were made to Anabaptist thought during these years. Two of these are lengthy answers to Schwenckfeld's attack on their *Confessional Book*. A third is a book that was published prior to 1550 and bears the title *Exposition of the Testament*, being a topical concordance compiled to assist them in their answers to Schwenckfeld. Its publication without indication of authorship and place created some stir among the authorities, especially when it was revealed that Marpeck had his own printing press.[4]

The major concerns of Marpeck during these years were to cut back the influence of the spiritualists among the Anabaptists, to rally the Swiss Brethren to his cause, and to maintain firm but loving discipline within his own group. The relative success of the latter particularly gives us reason to refer to the establishment of the Marpeck brotherhood as a binding and loosing community. Earlier we have observed that such passages as Matthew 18 were of crucial importance to the Swiss Anabaptists as well as to Hubmaier and other leaders. Schleitheim refers to the order of the spirit and in Marpeck's thinking as well, the function of the community as a binding and loosing one recurs at a number of places. He could not visualize the church as a church if it did not exercise this function.

It is therefore misleading to assume that because Marpeck rejected what he considered to be the legalistic approach of some of his fellow Anabaptists he did away with meaningful discipline. Indeed, a document has been preserved for us written by Helena von Freyberg which is a confession made to the assembled Anabaptists. The exact nature of her sin is not described, but the content of the document indicates clearly that mutual rebuke was practiced by the Marpeck brotherhood and at times was eminently effective in helping people experience forgiveness from their transgressions.

Marpeck's relevance for our discussion can be summarized under four points:

1. Within the Anabaptist tradition Marpeck is the only major thinker who worked consciously with both a Pauline and a Johannine orientation. Robert Friedmann has reminded us that the Anabaptists tended to live in the Sermon on the Mount, 1 Peter and James. This is certainly not true of Marpeck who found his major themes in Paul and in

---

4. Klassen, *Covenant and Community*, 51–53.

John. He felt at ease dealing with Pauline justification by faith and still remaining an Anabaptist who stressed discipleship.

2. The Marpeck group developed a non-legalistic ethic, yet it was not a formless ethic. In his fight against spiritualism Marpeck refused to concede to formlessness or an ethic of pure disposition. To be Christian you must stress external freedom. He stressed freedom, but in Christ. It was freedom to be obedient rather than to be disobedient.

3. On the issue of church unity Marpeck spoke in extremely clear and emphatic tones. His encounters with Bucer led him to see the value and importance of church unity on the wider Protestant basis. In some ways he sought to do for the Anabaptists what Bucer tried to do for Protestantism. He worked untiringly in his efforts to unite the Anabaptists, but at the same time he sought again and again to converse with the wider Reformation, particularly with Bucer. In addition to this people close to him began negotiations with the Moravian Brethren in an attempt to look at the differences between them as early as 1529. He took seriously John 17:11, stressing especially the point that unity to be real must be more than spiritual.

4. One cannot read Marpeck without being struck by the way in which he treated the wholeness of the Christian mission. The Hutterites stressed teaching and skills in the crafts and had some of the best-known physicians of their time. Marpeck, perhaps influenced by Paracelsus, early developed an interest in physical problems and in his letters occasionally offered prescriptions for maladies: "These herbs have been found helpful, I therefore recommend." Perhaps we are inclined to see in this an element of medical quackery but it should be remembered that over 90 percent of medical practice prior to 1900 was restricted to the placebo effect and that the great advance made in the sixteenth century was to actually prescribe herbs, rather than to pray or invoke the name of the Lord for every illness.

Conclusion

It must be pointed out that the Anabaptist-Mennonite faith has been virtually untouched by Marpeck's life and thought. The inaccessibility of his writings, the obscurity of his literary style, and perhaps the basic thrust of his message has made it easy for us to neglect him. Thanks to men like J. C. Wenger and Harold Bender we now take Marpeck seriously. His extant literary works exceed those of Menno eight to one. As a theologian he tackled the major issues raised in the sixteenth century. His answers are not always acceptable. Yet those who would emulate the Anabaptist faith could learn much from his emphasis on freedom—a freedom which comes by placing oneself under the guidance of God's Holy Spirit. We would do well to let him remind us again that the essence of Anabaptism lies not in such matters as the color of a coat or even the nonswearing of an oath but in the extent to which we allow the new life of Christ to be formed within us. Especially we may be allowed to suggest that Marpeck can teach us that nothing is to be lost by sitting down with fellow Christians to discuss our view of the Christian life. When such discussion does not take place within the Mennonite Brotherhood, we dare not call ourselves followers of Marpeck or of the Swiss Brethren for at the heart of the binding and loosing community is the practice of dialogue, discussion, or mutual exhortation. We have nothing to lose but our sins from such a process.

4.4

Anabaptist Studies 4

The State and Its Place: Rebellion and Rebuke

WILLIAM KLASSEN

Münster

In our study of Anabaptism, we have noted that as early as 1525 the Anabaptists developed a congregational structure growing out of their view of the church which made them less dependent upon the controls and protection of the state. While Anabaptists at several points had dealings with such revolutionary figures as Thomas Müntzer, the issue of the state and its role came to its most inflammatory point in the city of Münster. During the years 1532 to 1535 it became a center of radical Anabaptists. Special political, social, and religious conditions of the city made this possible. The city was ruled by a council and a bishop who had his own court. During the sixteenth century the guilds participated actively in public affairs and in government, leaving the common people very much in the background. By 1527 B. Knipperdolling had become the leader of the masses in their desire for improvement in economic, social, and religious conditions.

With the coming of Bernhard Rothmann to the city in 1531 the religious unrest of the city received considerable stimulation and guidance. He was a former priest who had visited Wittenberg and Strasbourg, having sought especially at the latter place to get a program on how to establish a religious government in a city. He was Lutheran and proclaimed that kind of message even in spite of the attempts of the authorities to stop him. He was supported by the powerful guilds of the city. A confession of faith published in 1531 reveals as yet no fanatic tendencies. In part because of his competent leadership the masses rallied around his cause and by August 10, 1532, all of the churches except the main cathedral were occupied by evangelical ministers. The guilds and the common people were clearly taking over and the council of bishops was losing out. Gradually the reform movement here divided into two major camps, the conservative Lutheran group and the democratic Sacramentarian wing which was ready to accept Anabaptist ideas.

The actual appearance of Anabaptist ideas in Münster came via East Friesland and the Netherlands where they had been widespread since 1531. Criticism of Catholic and Lutheran practices had been widespread in Münster but with the proclamation and practice of believer's baptism a new reform movement was introduced into Münster. On August 7–8, 1533, a religious discussion was held between the group of ministers adhering to Anabaptist ideas and Catholic and Lutheran ministers. Those who were inclined toward Anabaptist innovations were directed by the city council to baptize their children. Rothmann was removed from his office. He published his confession on the two sacraments, later used by Marpeck, on November 8, 1533. It bears the signatures of five other ministers and is dated October 22, 1533. It should be noted that at this time Rothmann himself was not an Anabaptist, although he sharply criticized the practice of infant baptism. In this confession he defines baptism "as dipping into water, which the candidate desires and receives as a true sign that he has died to sin, been buried with Christ, and arises in a new life, henceforth to walk not in the lust of the flesh, but obediently according to the will of God." Rothmann, along with a number of others, was baptized on January 5, 1531, by followers of Melchior Hoffmann. At about the same time John van Leyden appeared in Münster and peaceful Anabaptism gradually grew into a caricature. In October 1534, Rothmann published a book in which he urged the restitution of the apostolic church. On February 9, 1534, the city hall was seized and two weeks later Knipperdolling became mayor of Münster. On February 27 all those who refused to be baptized were expelled from the city. Phillip of Hesse sent two men to Münster to restore evangelical order, but they had to leave without accomplishing the task. Münster now became the refuge of all persecuted, desperate people, and "the new Jerusalem" of radical Anabaptism. Evangelists moved out spreading the news that the Lord had chosen Münster to establish his kingdom on earth. Many of the severely oppressed Dutch Anabaptists who were suffering greatly under Catholic authorities considered this message as coming directly from God. Many fled from Amsterdam and other cities across the Zuider Zee en route to the "New Jerusalem." Many were arrested and returned to their homes, others were imprisoned, many even put to death. Others were prevented by their local magistrates from leaving their home community. Nevertheless, large numbers succeeded in reaching Münster.

At the same time Bishop Franz of Waldeck, ruler of this area, initiated a siege of the city. Before this event, however, the original Anabaptist principle of nonresistance had been weakened through the fanatical view that the "children of Jacob" would be actively engaged in helping God punish and annihilate "the children of Esau" at the time of the establishment of the kingdom of God. Jan Matthys, a fanatical representative of this view, on April 4, 1534, followed a foolish inspiration to go outside the city walls to disperse the besieging army as had been done in days of old by the children of Israel. After he fell in this foolish attempt John van Leyden took his place in the city and cleverly exploited the situation. He appointed twelve elders to rule the city. In December 1534, Rothmann published an appeal for revenge and tried to defend the church of Christ at Münster. Another unusual incident showing how closely these people lived in the Old Testament concerns Hille Feicken, who sacrificed her life in an attempt to kill the bishop in the same way that Judith had beheaded Holofernes in Israel. She was captured and killed.

Not only did they resort to armed resistance but the practice of community of goods was soon instituted. The pattern probably was taken from the Jerusalem church as described in Acts.

John van Leyden also introduced polygamy against the judgment of some of the more serious ministers, including Rothmann. Originally it probably was an impulse of the "king of the new Zion." In the new Jerusalem in which the children of light were fighting the children of darkness "King David" could with the same justification introduce this Old Testament practice. At the same time polygamy served as a social welfare practice since the number of men continued to decrease during the siege of the city. John van Leyden had as one of his wives the widow of Jan Matthys, another wife was the daughter of Knipperdolling. Here then we are confronted with a perversion of Anabaptism through the fanaticism of certain people and we find a carnal, Old-Testament oriented, earthly kingdom of God. Very little of the early visions, spirit, and essence of Anabaptism were retained.

How did this come to pass? That is a question which deserves to be answered. Some would say that the ruthless persecution to which the Anabaptists were exposed in the Low Countries could produce only fanaticism among people who had no leaders. Even though the leaders made every attempt to recruit more helpers, it was only a matter of time until they were brutally defeated by the besieging forces. The behavior of John van Leyden in the last few days would seem to indicate that we are dealing here with a man who had delusions of grandeur and was completely misreading the Old Testament. Indirectly one of the positive results of Münster was the decision of Menno Simons to throw in his lot with these poor misguided fanatics and provide them with leadership. The two issues which seem to arise for discussion from these tragic events are the state and its limits and the place of the Old Testament.

The Place of the State

It has been common to describe the Anabaptist position on the state as one of withdrawal or noninvolvement. Hans Hillerbrand has recently published a well-documented study of the political ethics of South German Anabaptism. Perhaps the best term to describe the Anabaptist position on the matter of the state would be *apolitie*. From our studies so far, it is clear that the Anabaptists were concerned that decisions which belong in the church not be made by the state. This is not to say, however, that they did not recognize a legitimate realm for the state. As Schleitheim already says, outside of the perfection of Christ the state has its place. This means that we should not expect the government to conduct itself according to the Sermon on the Mount and that Christians would not be surprised when it resorts to force. On the other hand, the limits to which the Christian goes in his involvement in the state are also circumscribed because of the priority of other loyalties. The question was debated at considerable length whether a Christian could be a magistrate. We recall that Schleitheim took a clear position on it and ruled out this possibility. The South Germans on this point again seem to be somewhat more flexible, Marpeck stating that it is extremely difficult for a Christian to be a magistrate, perhaps even so difficult that we would have to admit that it is impossible, while others simply leave this question to God. However, certain Swiss Anabaptists also took the same position. Apparently, there is no definite statement ruling out the possibility of a Christian assuming the role of a magistrate. On the use of the sword the major position certainly was that a Christian could not kill for self-defense or any other reason. On the oath, likewise, the general Anabaptist position was that it was rejected.

Thus, the developments at Münster can be considered only as drastic perversions of that which is essential to Anabaptism. According to the major writers the state is ordained of God, it deserves our support by way of taxes and above all intercessory prayer, but it can never be given ultimate allegiance nor used to promote the kingdom of God. Where the interests of the state and those of Christ conflict, which may be more often than we are inclined to admit, Christ alone receives our loyalty.

The Old Testament

The Anabaptists were sometimes accused of rejecting the Old Testament as Scripture. Because they categorically rejected the circumcision-baptism analogy so important for the retention of infant baptism and because they refused to allow the Old Covenant ethic to attenuate that of the New, it was assumed that the Old Testament was not a part of their Bible. Evidence that any Anabaptist leaders rejected the Old Testament Scriptures has yet to be adduced.

To be sure, Leonhard Schiemer, and possibly others, cautioned their followers to read primarily the New Testament, but this in itself may already be a reaction to the preoccupation with the Old Testament seen in men like Thomas Müntzer and later the Münsterites. Thomas Müntzer picked up the militant strand of the Old Testament while Augustine Bader and the Münsterites succumbed to a strict biblicism of the Old Testament which had disastrous results. It hardly needs to be pointed out that these aberrant groups have no claim to be considered as Anabaptists, even though the assertion is at times made that their attitude toward the Old Testament is Anabaptist.

What then is the Anabaptist attitude toward the Old Testament? It is obvious that it is not uniform. An Anabaptist leader like Hans Denck thought it worthwhile enough to translate part of it from the Hebrew and thus made a significant contribution to the history of the German Bible. Others felt an affinity to the prophetic strains in the Old Testament. The *Ausbund*, a hymnbook, and the *Martyrs Mirror* borrow heavily from the narratives of the Old Testament, as does also the recently discovered *Codex Geiser*.

The Decalogue and the ethics of the Old Testament form the difficult portions and here there is less unanimity. Early this lack of unanimity comes to the surface in the formation of a group of Anabaptists who were Sabbatarians, led by the influential Oswald Glait. This Sabbatarian party lived on for some time and is evidence that a group of Anabaptists took the Decalogue so seriously that they tried to keep the one commandment which is not explicitly set aside by the New Testament church. Marpeck took a firm stand against this Sabbatarian party and insisted that no day of rest must be prescribed to the Christian.

One of the striking things about Marpeck's usage of the Old Testament is that he apparently used it as much as the New when the occasion demanded. In the *Confession*, his writing addressed to the Strasbourg Council (1532), he refers to the New Testament six times as often as to the Old; the ratio in the first part of the *Verantwortung* (1544) is eight to one, but in the second part (1550) it is three to two. In the *Testamenterleutterung* where it is his studied purpose to discuss the relationships between the two Testaments, he uses them about equally. As in the case of Irenaeus, so Isaiah is his favorite prophet and the book of Leviticus in the Pentateuch. In the New Testament Marpeck quotes most often from John and Paul, thus providing an exception to the assertion of Robert Friedmann that the Anabaptists lived primarily in the Synoptics and James and not in Paul and John.

In Marpeck's usage the Pentateuch and the Prophets stand out. In contrast to the *Ausbund* and martyr literature which used the narratives and the Psalms, Marpeck used the historical material and the prophetic material. His estimate of the Old Testament may be illustrated by examining some of the recurring themes he drew from the Old Testament.

The Old Testament as Preparation

During Marpeck's stay in Strasbourg, one of the complaints he lodged against the state churches was that the gospel was preached without any preaching of the law. In this respect Marpeck shows himself to be a true follower of Luther who also held to the position that one should not preach the gospel without first proclaiming the condemning law. First the law must reprove sin before the gospel could come with its healing. The Old Testament accordingly is given a preparatory role. The function of the law in specific is to bring knowledge and conviction of sin. How can a man come to the gospel unless he is first convicted by the law? asks Marpeck.

The stress Marpeck lays upon the law must be understood alongside the emphasis he places upon the fall and its consequences. He insisted that knowledge or awareness of sin comes only through the act of committing a sin. Adam's sin caused man to inherit a proclivity or tendency toward sin, but this is not considered guilt in the sight of God. Only the exercise of the will results in sin, and the atonement of Christ covers the innocent children and idiots.

In this view the awakening of the consciousness of sin becomes important, forming the necessary prelude to the acceptance of redemption. Within this context Marpeck defines the role of the law as increasing the sorrows of humanity. While sorrow ruled until the time of Moses the giving of the law through Moses only increased sorrow and grief because man was merely forced back upon an earnest petition to God for help. Before the coming of Christ man could not experience full forgiveness of sins and he could only be comforted by using the ceremonies which God had ordained for that purpose. The ancients of the Old Testament possessed a proleptic piety, they desired to do good, but their desires were frustrated by their lack of ability to act according to their desires. These desires were as shadows which pointed forward to the light which was coming in Jesus Christ.[1]

This was also the role played by John the Baptist. John preached repentance, revealed sin to men, and pointed them to Jesus. Marpeck refused to identify John's baptism with Christian baptism as was the vogue with the Reformers. In reply to Hubmaier's statement of the Anabaptist position Zwingli had argued that there is no difference at all between the two baptisms, and that repentance was all that was necessary for Christian baptism. It was argued with fervor that the New Testament knew nothing at all about rebaptism. How did they explain the apparent rebaptism of the disciples in Acts 19? Bucer insisted that since there is no such thing as rebaptism, neither by Christ, who was satisfied with John's baptism, nor by his disciples, the allegedly rebaptized disciples in Acts 19 in actuality did not receive the baptism of John. If they had they would have known about the Holy Spirit, according to Luke 3:16.

Since it is the nature of the law to increase the knowledge of sin, a corollary of its action is that grace also increases and takes the upper hand. Consequently, the Old Covenant can also be called the "first grace." In affirming the preexistence of Christ Marpeck does not rule out the activity

---

1. Marpeck, "Pilgram Marpeck's Confession," 177.

of Christ in the Old Covenant, but he distinguishes between Christ the preexistent and *Jesus* Christ who appeared in history. Until the coming of the son of God himself no full redemption was possible. Christ is the physician who heals those who through the law have been "crushed, broken, and pierced."[2]

The Old Covenant can also be called the first birth, in contrast to the other two births in the Old and New Testaments. This first birth brings with it the dead letter in two tablets of stone, signifying the hard demands of God. Honestly looking at himself, man sees that he can never meet the demands. They are too difficult, and he cannot keep them. Man is driven to despair and to rely on God's mercy and the only thing that makes the situation bearable is God's promise of Christ. According to Marpeck, Paul calls this first birth that of servitude.[3]

This stress on the negative preparation of the law for the coming of Christ Marpeck finds in Rom 7 and may have been prompted by his extensive disagreements with Bucer on the place of the Old Testament. The amount of emphasis already placed on the radical difference between Old and New Covenant in the *Confession* of 1532 is striking. The same stress is seen also in Marpeck's two other booklets of 1531, but there the trend of the discussion is quite different. There he also emphasized that the disciples did not have the Holy Spirit until after Pentecost, but the use of the Old Testament is extensive with the slightly self-conscious explanation that since the opponents use the Old Testament so much he will reply on their terms. The hermeneutical issue was different when dealing with spiritualizers, be they Schwenckfelders or of the Kautz-Bünderlin type.

The spiritualizers applied the words of 2 Cor 3, "The letter kills, but the spirit gives life," to any letter, even that of the New Testament. To this both Marpeck and Scharnschlager objected because this would cut the motivating nerve of New Testament preaching. They both applied it exclusively to the Old Testament.

Furthermore, the whole problem of the place of the letter or the law in the New Covenant is involved. Marpeck criticized the Hutterians for using pressure (*zwang*) to get people to relinquish private property and insisted that the New Testament had no law that property ought to be held in common. As recent discoveries show, however, his most serious disagreements

---

2. "Zerslagen, zerschnitten, und zerbrochen." Marpeck, "Pilgram Marpeck's Confession," 181.

3. Marpeck, "Pilgram Marpeck's Confession," 186–88.

on the question of legalism in the Christian life came from the side of the "Swiss Brethren." Correspondence has come to light in the last decade which shows clearly that there were deep disagreements between a certain group of Swiss Brethren in the St. Gall–Appenzell area and Marpeck. The Swiss accused Marpeck and his followers of being too free; Marpeck in turn complained that the Swiss congregations were so zealous that they had every leader under the ban, and some of them were under the double ban. What were the concrete issues? Between George Maler, a close associate of Marpeck, and the Swiss, they were something like this: Is it right to wear or weave bright-colored clothes? Maler said it was all right. The Swiss did not. The Swiss contended that one should not punish his wife, but Maler felt that this was carrying nonresistance one step too far. A wife is like a child and in need of discipline at times. Maler rejected the Swiss absolutism on not carrying a sword and also felt that the marriages ought to be reported to the government.

For Marpeck the issues were clear. The Christian man is a free man and is bound to Christ and his community. Marpeck's stature is seen in that he refused to become reactionary when he broke with Luther but tried desperately hard in his own brotherhood to steer a middle course between the libertinism in the Strasbourg Anabaptist brother hood and the legalism of the Swiss Brethren. Fortunately, Marpeck's clear conception and devotion to Paul's gospel and the description of the Christian life assisted him in steering this course. He retained church discipline, but it is always clearly redemptive in approach; he practiced controlled communion, but he had none of the marks of the moralist who is so well portrayed in the parable of the Pharisee and the publican in the Gospels. Was he right in throwing the law out of court as far as the Christian life is concerned? On the basis of Paul, one is inclined to say, "Yes." The past four hundred years have also shown that the answer which he gave should not be ignored, even though it is admittedly easy to slip back into the comfortable routine of legalism and thus deny one's sonship. Marpeck's ideal of the Christian life where the Christian is guided not by any legalistic biblicism but by the Spirit working through the body of believers in the church may be a more dangerous ethical ideal—but no one has yet shown on the basis of the New Testament that this is not precisely what Paul was describing. While Scharnschlager, his close co-worker, explicitly advocated *sola fideism* this did not mean that the Christian common life does not take recognizable form. Such a form is given by the living historical Christ himself.

For Marpeck the law had a provisional preparatory role. Once you are in Christ the law is gone, and the Christian is driven on by the Spirit. This is one of the favorite images used by Marpeck—the driving of the Spirit. To keep this from degenerating into any subjective individualism Marpeck insisted that each motive, each drive of the Spirit be shared in the community of the Spirit where it would receive correction and purification. Those who did not subject themselves to this because of pride or other deficiency were disciplined as the case of Helene von Freyberg clearly shows.

Marpeck stressed the discontinuity between the two Covenants rather than the continuity. It should be observed however that he saw his position as a corrective one. The Reformers read the New Testament back into the Old while the Anabaptists themselves were always in danger of dragging the law back in through the back door. Fighting on both of these fronts and seeing the tragic results of a fanatic devotion to the Old Testament at Münster, Marpeck resigned himself to a usage of the Old Testament which placed high value on the devotional use of the Song of Solomon. (And here he is following the great mystics, notably Bernard of Clairvaux, although Origen, Ambrose, and many other commentators exegeted the Songs.) For Marpeck, in contrast to the mystics, the bride was always the church, never the individual. For this and other reasons he does not belong among the mystics.

Did Marpeck overemphasize the difference between the Old and New Testament? Undoubtedly. We do not accept his statements today and we have every right to criticize Marpeck for stressing so much the difference between Abraham and the Christian that he fails to adequately note that the element that ties them together is faith-obedience—a good Pauline point. He allowed his opponents to force him too far in making assertions about the salvation of the patriarchs and there are few who will follow him in the devious paths taken to get himself off the exegetical hook!

Let us pose a final question: Was he Marcionite? It depends a good deal on what we mean by Marcionite. What the church condemned about Marcion was not only his aversion to the Old Testament (for then there are many Marcionites today!) but basically his cleavage of the Godhead into an angry and a compassionate God. Of this there are only traces in Marpeck. This is the more impressive because there are numerous Marcionite leanings in Marpeck; for example, the incident on the way to Jerusalem where Jesus refused to have fire come down from heaven on the Samaritans, a passage which Marpeck loved to quote and so did Marcion. Indeed, one of the firmest textual supports for Jesus's reply: "Know ye not what spirit ye are?" (Luke 9:55) comes from the hand of Marcion.

Another just as striking is the assertion by Marcion that Jesus did not merely go to Hades to proclaim his victory over death, but actually to proclaim forgiveness and offer salvation to the patriarchs. Between Marpeck and Schwenckfeld this was a recurring cause for contention, Marpeck maintaining that Jesus actually gave salvation to the patriarchs at that time, while Caspar Schwenckfeld argued that Jesus merely announced his victory to them then. The publication of several editions of the *Gospel of Nicodemus* in German in Augsburg in 1525 and after would lead one to suspect that some Anabaptists, and Marpeck may surely have been among them, read this booklet and thereby were sped on their way to reflect, not too productively to be sure, on how Christ spent the three days between his death and his resurrection. If Marpeck is to be accused of being Marcionite *in tendency*, this would be a difficult charge to rebut, and possibly the best one could do would be to take comfort in that Martin Luther too has been accused of this.

One fundamental point at which Marpeck is not Marcionite is in his view of history and human development. While Marcion and Schwenckfeld, Bünderlin and Bucer (and even some of the Reformers) but especially Sebastian Franck made much of the fact that humanity had not been ready in the Old Testament for the New, it was still too childish, but now we are ready to move beyond the infantile stages of the Old, Marpeck never accepted this position. He insisted that God's manner of dealing with man in history is determined by his sovereignty and not by man's progressive evolution. One needs only think of Harnack's Neomarcionitism to see that this position has considerable relevance for today. According to Marpeck we return again and again to the Old Testament and we never say that we have grown beyond using it, because it forms an organic part of God's whole dealing with mankind.

Finally, what relevance does this have for modern theology? H. Richard Niebuhr has recently stated: "The relationship of the Old Testament to the New is a central issue in biblical studies, and in the interpretation of the nature of Christianity." This is certainly correct. In the ecumenical discussions about the lordship of Christ, this issue was also isolated as needing further attention. H. H. Wolf in his study of Calvin's position on this matter admitted that Calvin's position may have only slight relevance for today for we will have difficulty accepting the answers as valid even when we accept the questions as such. The possibility of such irrelevance exists for each sixteenth-century answer given to this issue.

In Marpeck's case, however, it is hard to consider his solution to the problem as irrelevant when we notice that he finds the element of continuity between the Old and the New in the covenant-making God, and we find some of the best Old Testament scholars doing the same today. When that which binds Old and New together is promise and fulfillment, we approach the position of Friedrich Baumgärtel. The differences are admittedly great, yet the similarities may be even more significant.

Our study of this problem, however, is motivated on a deeper level than merely to find surface differences and similarities. The Reformation discussions on this subject should lead us to strive for a measure of consistency in our approach to the Old Testament which was strikingly absent then. Calvin, while he argued for substantial identification of the two covenants, refused to allow the women to adorn themselves with jewels just because Rebecca did. And the statement that Jacob kissed Rachel before introducing himself to her so profoundly shocked his "puritan" standards that he averred that there must be a textual transposition (Gen 29:11). In actual fact Jacob probably introduced himself first and then kissed Rachel.

In the area of ethics Christianity has had most difficulty relating the two covenants and it is apparent that this is the area in which discussion is most needed. Precisely because Marpeck's position clearly distinguishes between Old and New Testament ethics, and because he took God's action in history seriously, and because he was able to avoid both legalism and libertinism, his voice may still deserve our attention.

Jan J. Kiwiet argues that in spite of the fact that Marpeck was not a trained theologian (perhaps because of it) he appears to be much closer to the Hebraic thought-forms of the Bible than many of the major Reformers who were bound to Aristotelian patterns of thought. Schwenckfeld was clearly tied to Neoplatonism which he received via Augustine. This is even more true of Bünderlin and Franck. In his rejection of the distinction between the Word and the Spirit Marpeck also affirms the importance of history as the area in which God works. Having committed himself to this point of view he could not depreciate the Old Testament except insofar as it was depreciated by God's greatest act in Jesus Christ. His position cannot therefore be accepted or rejected without study. It needs to be tested by the way in which biblical writers themselves view the relationship between Old and New Covenants. His position is clearly worthy of such a test.[4]

---

4. Documentation for the position described here is found in Klassen, *Covenant and Community*, 101–48.

4.5

Anabaptist Studies 5

The Style of the New Life in Christ as Viewed in Anabaptist History and Theology

WILLIAM KLASSEN

The Center of Anabaptism

What I propose to do now is to take a look at a specific aspect of Anabaptist Mennonite thought, namely, ethics. Whether we should really speak of ethics in the technical classical sense is a debatable point, and it deserves more debate than it receives. Strictly speaking, we can hardly say that there is such a thing as a biblical ethic, if we use it in the way that it was first coined by the Greek thinkers. It has, however, a vigorous history in Christianity and other religions and therefore cannot be scrapped. The question which we want to pose here is: How did the faith of the Anabaptists and how does our faith express itself in the concrete dilemmas and decisions of life? Where do we get guidance on how these decisions are to be resolved? It seems to me that this was an urgent question among the early Anabaptists and still is for us today. We cannot evade it. Some people feel that the Anabaptists discussed ethics too much and allowed the ethical, the practical, the moral concern to dominate their whole thinking. They assert that the Anabaptists did not always provide an adequate Christological or theological base when they pursued the answer to this question. It may be, but it would be wrong to say that this is true of the total movement.

Already at Schleitheim (1527) the expression occurs, "walking in the resurrection," as Harold S. Bender observed in a paper read at the conference on the holy life. This conference was an interesting confrontation of the holiness tradition with the members of the Anabaptist family. Bender took this expression from Schleitheim as the clue to the Anabaptist view of the holy life. It is not then, apparently, an ethic patterned on the cross. This is not a crucifixion theology, but rather a resurrection theology. It is the resurrection which provides perspective. Now, of course, it is a cross-bearing ethic in the sense that the Christian is a disciple. But there is always a triumphant note in the Christian life which comes to expression in this formula from Schleitheim that we "walk in the resurrection."

There is another little pamphlet which ought to be reprinted in a modern tract form and distributed, entitled "On Two Types of Obedience." We don't know who wrote it, but it is clearly an Anabaptist tract. It may have been written by Sattler; it is dated early, around 1527, and its provenance is Swiss or South German. In this tract two types of obedience are put against each other and contrasted very sharply. The one type is a servile kind of obedience. In the parable of the prodigal son, the younger son concludes, "Well, it's pretty rough out here in the pigpens; I'm going to go home, and I'm going to get a job. I'm going to work for Dad and get my regular paycheck. My responsibilities will be clearly defined. I'll work forty hours a week for which I get $40 a week." This is a servile kind of obedience. Now you know that when the son comes home with this proposition, he is not even allowed to finish his sentence because God doesn't want people to serve him like that. When Henry Ford joined the Roman Catholic Church some years ago he was quoted in the press as having said that the reason he wanted to join the Catholic Church was that everything was clearly defined in the Roman Church as to what you should do. As a businessman he knows what a contract means. He makes a contract with the church. He does what they ask him to do, and then he should also get what they promise him.

This Anabaptist tract fights against such a view of servile obedience. Christ calls us to sonship. What is available to us in this new relationship is a state of sonship in which you relate yourself to God with both the responsibilities and the opportunities of being a son, not only a servant. This is a theme, incidentally, which is very prominent in Marpeck's writings also. In fact, he goes to the extreme of saying that Luther and some other people whom he names never really move from the level of servitude to the level of sonship. They have, therefore, never really experienced the freedom and the power of the gospel, because they still look upon God as something of a tyrant, a benevolent tyrant to be sure, and one that forgives as an indulgent figure, but never really as a father. So, at least, in some areas of the Anabaptist ethic they begin with this theme—the relationship of sonship; and man receives his dignity not from creation, although that, too, is there, but his dignity comes from the fact that God actually relates himself to him on this level.

But if we were to look at what seems a central theme of the Anabaptist ethic, one could perhaps describe it best with the term "newness." They lived in a new order. A very important text for them was: "the old has passed away." Everything that had come in Christ was new. There was a new source of life available in Christ; and if we look at it today, it is, of course, very hard for us to be objective in determining to what extent there really was this newness of life to which they gave such abundant testimony. There is a classic passage in Sebastian Franck's *Chronica* of 1531 which shows that he was impressed by the kind of life that they were living. It is quoted by John Horsch, Harold Bender, John Wenger, and other modern writers. They say, here is contemporary testimony to the way in which these people lived. Nor can we ignore it. There were other people who said the same thing. Bucer paid tribute to them often; and where the Hutterites lived, contemporary writers also paid tribute to them. So it seems that there was a quality of new life here which struck their contemporaries, which made an impression upon them. In an article called "The Sociology of Swabian Anabaptism," Claus-Peter Clasen concludes by saying that the reason why the Anabaptists could not win converts in Swabia was that they had such a rigorous ethic. The demands they made for change of life were so great that people felt they couldn't meet this standard.[1] Here then seems to be some quite direct evidence for the quality of this new life.

New Power

How can we formulate best what is involved here? It seems, first of all, there is a strong conviction that a new source of power has been made available

---

1. Clasen, "Sociology," 179.

to them. That man has a supernatural power which drives him on, that man is driven by the Holy Spirit, comes to clear expression in men like Marpeck and Hut and others. But, also, there is a source of power to change the old patterns of behavior and adopt new patterns in their place. Here, they said, is where the testimony to the resurrection of Christ finds its ultimate conclusive test. If you believe in it, it is not something which you simply repeat in the creed but something which changes your behavior. There is in the power of Christ's resurrection a radically new force to overcome evil. I do not believe that one can explain this movement without recognizing this conviction. I don't know whether you can ever explain any movement in history completely but, at least, you are missing a very important aspect of the Anabaptist movement if you omit this driving conviction of the new power which had come to them in Christ.

New Loyalty

But alongside of this sense of new power there was also a radical break with the old loyalties and a call to the new loyalties. In Bonhoeffer's book, *The Cost of Discipleship*, he comments on this strange verse in Luke 14:26 which has always been a very difficult verse to interpret. Matthew already provides an easier interpretation of it. The verse according to Luke reads: "When there was a great crowd assembled, and Jesus having turned to them said to them: 'If any man comes to me and is not hating his father and his mother, his wife and his children, his brothers and his sisters, yes, in fact, even his own life, he is not able to be my disciple.'" A student said in a discussion that she is afraid to walk through St. Louis because she likes her life. All of us do. But can you imagine anything more radical than this? There is no way that you can water this kind of verse down. The word stands there in a very bold form—hate. And Bonhoeffer, commenting on this, says that what Jesus is telling his disciples here is that if we were to draw a circle and place the ego at the center and outside of this ego, to some extent bound up with it, our relationships: the parental relationship, the sibling relationship, the spouse relationship, the children relationship, and then the relationship to one's own self, to his own ego, we would find that what Jesus is saying is that no relationship can exist except it go through Christ. Every loyalty to father, to mother, has to be sifted or screened through the loyalty to Christ. This is the ultimate, the most important loyalty. Now in a way we must say that this is just impossible.

When we see his statement, however, in the context of the world in which it was made there are interesting factors which cast light on it. There are battle formulas in which the Greek soldier was told: "Do not sign up for this battle, do not go into this war unless you hate father, mother," and so on. The call to arms was given with the assumption that it may cost you your life; and that it is really an expression of hatred to your wife to leave when you know full well that you may never return. Now it seems that Jesus says, no one can ask you to give up your life except I. There is an imperialistic demand here, an absolute claim, an ultimate loyalty which means a radical break with all other loyalties.

One should, of course, understand this in the language in which it was spoken, which was Aramaic. In Aramaic you only have the word "love" and its antonym "hate." There are no intermediate steps. In English we consider ourselves more fortunate. We can say, "I don't love that person, nor do I hate him, I merely like him." The language in which Jesus spoke did not have such an option available. There may also be something profoundly true about this beyond language itself. Suppose that a man is lying beside the road and I'm on my way uptown, and I see him lying there, but I'm in a very big hurry, so I just keep on going. How do I feel toward this man? I could try to convince myself that while I don't love him, nor like him, I certainly don't hate him either. But my expression of unconcern is really an act of hatred because I value my own affairs more deeply than I do his life or his comfort.

In the Old Testament some very illuminating passages use this word "hate." Jacob had two wives, one he loved and the other one he hated (Gen 29). In Deut 21:15 a legal formula occurs in which the person is told what to do with the children of the wife that is hated. A man has two wives, the one loved, the other hated; and the children of the hated wife are to be guaranteed certain privileges and certain access to the family farm. What we have here is simply a man who has a favorite wife, and the Hebrew "hated one" is not "the disliked one," as the RSV unfortunately translated it, but the Hebrew word is hate. The same thing is true of the verse in Mal 1:2, 3: "Jacob I loved, Esau I hated." You have only those two terms.

There is still something very important here for our own conception of what it means to be loyal to something. Is the youth who listens to his mother's plea that he should stay at home and take care of the family farm really better off than the one who says, "Duty calls me, Christ calls me, and I must leave"? Very often, of course, we say, to neglect parental responsibilities is a bad thing. Somebody ought to take care of those old folks; and in certain cases, maybe this is right. Yet there is much evidence of personalities that were really crippled because they were not able to say no to Dad and Mom and, likewise, Dad and Mom were crippled in their emotional development or in their service because they were overly dependent upon children. There is a profound truth here which indicates some overlap between Christ's call and modern psychology.

When we use this word "hate" we think in too restricted terms of psychological hate. We get our emotions all lathered up and we are red in the face. If we look at it, rather, in this sense that our act is an act of love and loyalty to Christ which is interpreted by the loved one, however, as an act of hate, we may be in a much better position. This is what the Anabaptists really did by looking at loyalty to Christ as primary. There were extremes here by some of the Anabaptists which need not detain us but at the center Luke's account of this word of Christ for one thing I think is more original than the one that we have in Matthew. Matthew says that if a man loves father and mother, and so on, "more than me." I think that is already a concession; it is a watering down in a way. But the main thing that this passage would tell us is that whenever we absolutize any of these other relationships, we tend to lose the best perspective in life. We find this with newly married couples who live on Cloud Nine and become completely absorbed in themselves, but over the years this relationship simply corrupts and loses its earlier glow because there is no outside interest. Where people find a good perspective outside of themselves, outside of their own family relationships, they find themselves in a purpose and do not absolutize these human relationships, life becomes much more significant and meaningful Christ tells us that there is only one absolute loyalty which can give meaning to life and that is to him.

This radical break with all other loyalties, this exclusive loyalty to Christ, characterizes the form of the new life in Christ as seen by the Anabaptists in its earliest forms. Since then we have radically changed this so that in most Mennonite communities, whether it be Goessel, Kansas, or Moundridge, or Halbstadt, Manitoba, the greatest thing that a person can do is stay at home and take over the family farm. If that is changing to some extent now, it is because of economic pressure, not theological insight or our view of discipleship. We ought to recognize not only the changes but the reasons which underlie them.

New Love

Third, the Anabaptist-Mennonite views the Christian life as a consistent expression of all-inclusive love. This is one of the weakest parts of our current Anabaptist ethic, partly because we have substituted nonresistance for biblical love. The word "nonresistance" does not occur in the New Testament. It is derived from the prohibition in the Sermon on the Mount, "do not resist the evil one," and is only, as far as I know, used at that one place.

To speak positively, however, according to Anabaptist-Mennonite faith, love is applied within the brotherhood. The repeated charge against the early Anabaptists that they were communists has a basis in their statements that all goods that belong to one belong equally to all the brothers. Now this has been radically carried out, first of all, by the Hutterites, who in the early part of the 1530s decided to implement community of goods in a very definite legalistic way, but at its basis there is a very good view of the world and stewardship here. Ambrosius Spittelmair and Hans Hut and others when accused of teaching communism said: We do not believe in community of goods, but we believe that we have everything in common. For the purposes of legality and order it is quite legitimate for one man to take out title on a farm or car, but if the brother comes and says, I have need of this car, or this farm, then you, of course, let him use it or share it with him. Now one could say that this is very naive and yet it comes from the conviction that "the earth is the Lord's" (Ps 24:1). We are tenants, and it is certainly no more radical than the jubilee arrangements in the Old Testament which provided for an equalizing in the jubilee year.

But what about the outsider, what about people who are outside of the group? Can love express itself consistently to them also? Well, as we know, the Anabaptists took the position very consistently that we must also love our enemies. It is really striking how far back the theme of loving one's enemy goes into the history of mankind. We have it clearly expressed for pragmatic grounds in some of the Egyptian literature. We have it in some of the texts of Stoics. It appears in a good deal of the older material, antedating the Old Testament, and we certainly have it in the Old Testament. Rom 12 is crucial here and we have not used it enough in our evaluation of the Anabaptist position. Paul moves there from the theological (he gives theology in the first eight chapters), then 9, 10, and 11 are history, using the common divisions of the material in that time. Then in chapter 12 he moves to exhortation with the word *parakaleo*, for which we use the technical term, *paranesis*, which really means to admonish people to now live out specifically in daily life the things that they have spoken of theoretically. If we take chapter 12 as a unit, the first paragraph is extremely important in understanding the whole passage and particularly the conclusion. The whole purpose of giving one's self to God, presenting the body, not just the soul and mind, but the body as a living sacrifice is that we may in our daily living experience God's good pleasure and be able to ascertain his will. The heart of the matter for us begins in verse 14. Paul says here that you do not pray only for the people with whom you have direct contact, but you pray for all the persecutors wherever they may be or bless them, which is even stronger. You can pray for them because goodness knows they need it, and hope they'll be converted and change their ways, but to ask God to bless them instead of curse them is a very radical departure from what most people do. Paul repeats bless and do not curse.

Verse 17 says "under no circumstances"—the Greek is very strong—

> under no circumstances repay evil for evil. Rather, take thought of, consider the good things in the presence of all men. If possible, as much as comes out of you, live peaceably, or establish peace among all men. Do not avenge yourselves, beloved, but rather give place to the wrath. for it stands written, to me is vengeance, I will repay, says the Lord. But if your enemy hungers, feed him. If he is thirsty, give him to drink, for by so doing you will heap coals of fire upon his head.

The next sentence gives us the clue for their whole view of overcoming evil in the Christian church, and this is one thing that Anabaptism was completely committed to. "Do not overcome the evil, or do not be overcome by the evil, but overcome evil by the good." Do not allow evil to have the victory but get the victory over the evil by the good. Now if you will analyze this strategy, you certainly cannot say that this is nonresistance. This is not passivity. Epictetus said if somebody comes and beats you, even as much as you'd beat a dog, bite your teeth together and love him as a brother. That is mighty noble. You receive a beating and you just bite your teeth and say, "I'll love him anyhow." In fact, this is what we've done very often. This is nonresistance. Just let them beat. I've got a tough skin. I can take this. But precisely this Paul does not say. In the presence of evil, you do not simply allow people to take advantage of you and to persecute you and do anything else. You pray for them; you bless them. That is, you are not repressing your hostilities or your anger at what they're doing to you; but you're taking another means to overcome it. Certainly you never tolerate evil. Evil has to be overcome—it can be overcome. Jesus showed us that on the cross. And so when the enemy comes, concretely, the man who hates you, who wants nothing more than your destruction—when he comes, you are prepared for him.

Here you have the whole question of vengeance. Paul says, do all you can to live at peace; but if that breaks down and somebody does something wrong, there is an outbreak of hostility, we might say, and you are tempted to take vengeance, don't do it. Give place to the wrath of God. Allow God to take his course of action. Incidentally, the quotes from the Old Testament are striking here. Who would ever say that Paul does not base his ethic on the Old Testament? But it is a selective basing; and those who have said or say that war can be justified from the Old Testament, or that killing can be justified from the Old Testament, should read this. If it can really be justified, why is it that it never seems to have entered the minds of Paul and Jesus? They never find in the Old Testament a license to kill under certain special occasions. When Jesus walked to the city of Samaria he was rejected, as they told him he couldn't stay in their town. The disciples said, "We have Old Testament precedent. Look what Elijah did when he was rejected. Call down fire from heaven. Let's do what Elijah did. Let's punish them." Each time the suggestion to base an ethic on the Old Testament, that you repay evil with evil, is turned aside. A new order has arrived. To be sure, the Old Testament has both sides in it. This is quite clear. As a follower of Christ, you don't just stand there and wait till God sends the coals of fire down, nor do you merely say: "He'll get his due; I'll just sweat it out waiting now for those people to get what they deserve."

Paul advocates, instead, an active program. You get busy and do something yourself. You don't leave everything to God, although you leave vengeance to him. But when the enemy is hungry, you give him something to eat, and you give him something to drink. In other words, you get rid of anger and overcome hostility by doing something positive about it by breaking down the resistance or the wall of hostility that exists between you and the enemy. These are very positive kinds of actions.

What confuses the issue is the last part of verse 20, "for thus you will heap coals of fire upon the head," and people say Paul certainly thinks that these people are going to get what they deserve because the only other place in the Old Testament where we read about coals of fire is in Sodom and Gomorrah, and in Ps 140:10, in which coals of fire are obviously meant to be destructive. Certain Old Testament commentators have said that Proverbs already talks about the worst possible kind of revenge that anyone can take, namely demolition. One religious editor argued that the United States should take the first blow and really let the coals of fire rain down upon the heads of our enemies. This is surely amateur exegesis. Since the archaeological work done in Egyptian religious rituals in the past sixty years, we have a clue to the understanding of this verse. For one thing, we must establish that the proverb, which he is here quoting, probably comes from Egypt. This is not too difficult because if you read Prov 25:21 you note that the north wind brings rain. Now this is not true of Palestine, and scholars have labored to figure out what this means. The usual way is to say that it doesn't really mean "brings" but "disperses," and it is true that the north wind tends to disperse rain in Palestine. Others say what he really means is the northwest wind brings rain in Palestine. The most satisfying alternative is to assume that, as many proverbs, this one has its provenance in Egypt, where it is true that the north wind brings rain. Now, if it has its location in Egypt, then we can tie it up with some very interesting religious rituals that have been discovered in the last few years in Egypt. One of these involves the carrying of burning coals upon the head. In some of this material we read of tensions and animosities, which came between two people. The narrative says that the one party had gone away in anger, and he came back to his adversary bearing a two-pronged staff in his hand and a platter of burning coals upon his head. These were the symbols of change of heart and mind, of the desire for reconciliation. It would be something like walking out with a white flag, a sign of surrender, although it doesn't have quite that connotation. Coals of fire are then an outward symbol of an inner change that has taken place.

Not all the difficulties of interpreting are thereby removed. Paul certainly didn't know about this Egyptian ritual, and yet the rabbis did not take this proverb in the punitive sense but took it in the sense of repentance. There is some evidence that the Septuagint translators knew about this Egyptian ritual so that it may have been more common than we think. At any rate, it is clear that in the world in which Paul lived a man with burning coals on his head did not have connotations of punishment. Coals were commonly carried on their heads.

When one looks at it in this way then Paul is saying that by doing this you are going to be an instrument of overcoming evil by good, you are repaying good for the evil which he gave you and in this way may change him from an enemy to a friend or from a pagan to a Christian. Whatever we may say about the details of this material, it is clear from the conclusion that Paul is talking about victory. He is not encouraging the Christian to overcome evil by withdrawing from the fight. Stay in and fight! But be careful about the kind of weapons that you use. And these weapons are very clearly described here in this whole chapter where the whole question of love and the active and powerful way in which it demonstrates itself in human affairs is treated.

More could be said about this, but it is quite clear that one of the marks of our tradition has always been the consistent way in which the ideal of love has been understood, and the importance that has been attached to it. One of the tragedies of our history is that Christianity has become so Stoicized. Perhaps this is one of the reasons why a Roman Catholic psychiatrist once said, "Depressed are the peace makers." If you cannot deal with hostility in a creative way, depression often results; and this is what has happened, not only to our culture but certainly often to our people. We have not taken a really creative approach to our hostilities and, therefore, have lost our joy. We have it in our heritage. It is certainly in the New Testament, but something has happened in history. We can't deal with all that, but we are in a position today to move beyond a negative nonresistance and have, in some areas, already moved beyond this and taken a more creative approach to the resolution of hostilities.

Christians Are Different

There is another conviction which pervades our tradition which is based with more or less sophistication upon the first two verses of Rom 12. It is the conviction which put simply is that Christians are different. There is a difference, and I think this is something that we ought to look at. We can laugh at the Swiss Brethren for saying to Rothenfelder, "The clothes have to be drab"; we can say this is wrong, ridiculous, naive; but we cannot laugh at the conviction which has at times been at the heart of this concern, namely, that Christians are different. They *are* different. They live in a world which is not Christian, and which never will be Christian, as far as we know. There is certainly very little hope. When you look at the history of Israel, why should we say that the world today will not repeat the mistake that Israel made—the mistake of rebellion?

How is this difference between church and world to be defined? This is really one of the big issues that confront us in our heritage today. We pay lip service to the fact that Christians are different, but we have not defined this in a specific way. Materialism is just as serious as conformity to the world, whether we have it in Souderton or Lancaster, or Manitoba, or anywhere. How strange it is that we would argue, and many do, that to be a Mennonite you have to wear plain clothes, or you have to speak German, when the real issue is really being evaded. The difference between a Christian and a non-Christian, a Mennonite and a non-Mennonite, is on the level of values. One of the most striking discoveries was made by Frank Peters when he studied the values of some of our young people and discovered, among other things, that there is virtually no difference in values between those who attend church schools and those who do not. If we're not changing people's values in our schools, then what in the world are we doing?

After this historical sketch let us look at some specific issues which confront us as Mennonites today. We have some homework to do first. There are some cardinal points of our heritage which are sadly missing today. Radical love is often changed to passive nonresistance, the conviction that Christians are different is often changed into a sterile conception of nonconformity. My favorite article in *The Mennonite Encyclopedia* is the one on suspenders. When suspenders first came in, they were considered new and modern, so some said they were of the world. Anything that's new is of the world, is worldly, and people who want to wear suspenders and snap them are just proud. So they had nothing to do with suspenders and proved that trousers could be kept up by less worldly means. There was a second party, of course, who said, "They are new and they're certainly utilitarian and so we'd like to wear them." They did. They went all out and wore suspenders. There was a third group which said, "You can't have it all. It's not all good and it's not all bad so we'll make a compromise and wear one suspender." This is a good example of what has happened in our tradition, and not only in our tradition, it happens in other traditions, too. Today we might assume that the people who wear suspenders are conservative although a really conservative man is one who wears both a belt and suspenders!

This is an illustration of what happens to us when we say what is new is bad, what is old is good. Paul never says that. Look in the whole New Testament, especially these first few verses of Rom 12. Paul doesn't say your nonconformity to the world should be expressed by looking at the new very critically. The basic question he assumes is the will of God. The same thing is true of First John where he urges his readers not to love the world. The key question is: "What is the will of God?" If you do that, you'll endure forever. If you don't, you won't. We have so often asked the wrong question on this point.

The same is true on believer's baptism. We have lost contact with our heritage. Very few of us really had believer's baptism. When you take seriously the fact of the Mennonite who originated in Russia because they wanted believer's baptism, it stands as a judgment over us. We cannot lose believer's baptism and still really be a part of the Anabaptist tradition. The same thing is true of *koinonia*, a word that we've heard so much, fellowship. To a very large extent we've lost it. Not that we ought to take old patterns and reinstitute them. What happens so often to us is that we lose the old and don't replace it. We don't even (as the Amish) have two Sundays a month to visit. When we visit with the members of the church, our friends, what do we talk about? So often trivialities, not the things that really burn at the center of our being. It is strange—the kind of life we live today—when one can't really build on deep levels of fellowship. Life is so superficial.

Yet there is hope. In fact, one of the real signs of hope is that there has been a real recovery of the Anabaptist vision. We can quibble about terms here, but I lose my pessimism when I work in the church and see the way in which people do change their ways of thinking. We have found more creative ways of expressing our position on love, and we have discovered that when you start teaching something passionately and consistently and thoroughly people change their ways of thinking, and our young people are taking this much more seriously now than they did twenty years ago. We have seen in our own twentieth century that intensive and courageous leadership pays off at the grass roots. We sometimes hear among the church and the politicians that we can't get ahead of our people. But these same people, these same leaders, have often been the ones who, when they took a position with courage, could bring their whole denomination with them and convince them that this is really what God wants us to do today. Dean Bender certainly did it on discipleship. He did it on his view of nonresistance.

It has been one of the most interesting things to study Mennonite history and note the way in which some of these changes have come in. Clayton Beyler discovered that no place in Anabaptist history was 1 Cor 11 ever connected with a specific headgear, but that about 1860–1870 the leadership of one group of Mennonites began to join these two and began to stress it. The main reason that it became so firmly entrenched was that they needed specific reason for existence apart from other Mennonite groups. At about the same time came the reaction against jewelry. The use of utilitarian jewelry was standard until about 1920. When Daniel Kauffman and the revival came, part of this revival was to get rid of all jewelry, including wedding rings. When we look at the origin of these peculiar practices and see them within our own history, we get a completely different perspective than if we simply assume that's what the New Testament says and, therefore, that's what we ought to do.

When we read George Williams's *The Radical Reformation* and other books, we discover that the term "the radical Reformation" may be a good way to describe our Anabaptist forefathers. To what extent does this radical element carry over for us today?

Perhaps I should say something about resources. I am impressed by the intellectual resources we have. There is a tremendous resource here. Sometimes we get angry at our parents for having taught us to work hard, that we feel guilty because we're not working right now, and because we have been taught that one ought to be doing something all the time, and we get angry about it and wonder why we have to have guilt feelings about not working. Take for a moment the other alternative. The question of motivation is one of the most difficult ones to solve. Hard as the psychiatrist may be on people who really teach their children the values of hard work, the other alternative is pretty sickening. You see them all the time: children from wealthy homes, well-educated homes, who have never been motivated, don't care to do a thing. Our tradition has its weaknesses and its dangers, but there is yet to appear a valid alternative, a good one.

We also have tremendous financial resources, and I'm always a little uneasy when some of our people feel guilty about the wealth we have in our church. We should feel guilty, perhaps, about the fact that we don't give more, but it seems to me that wealth should be seen simply as a gift of God. We can't help it that we are living in prosperous America. Let's simply take it as a gift of God and use it as such without allowing guilt to drive us or cripple us in the exercise of this stewardship.

We have tremendous spiritual resources. There is a depth of commitment which is hard to understand. A number of people have asked me, how could you ever get so many university students to come out here for two weeks? What drives these people? How much did you pay them? I don't want to flatter you, but this is surely evidence of the kind of concern that we have among our young people to really ask spiritual questions, and spiritual in the deepest sense, not merely getting your glands all lathered up or anything like that. Spiritual in the sense that you're asking about ultimate reality and about the relationship of the work that you're doing to the God who is spirit and who can be worshiped only in spirit and in truth. Before us lies, however, a tremendous task. We need to recover our mission and there are a number of ways in which we could do this. We could return, for example, to our Anabaptist past and say that the Anabaptists never really fitted, they didn't belong to the magisterial reformation, they didn't belong to the Roman Church, they didn't belong to the spiritualists, they didn't belong to the humanists, they just didn't fit. And, as you know, some have argued that we ought to join the National Council of Churches and we ought to at least get to the point where we can talk to other Christians in some arena someplace. They feel that our light, our position, will not suffer by being exposed to other positions. Certainly, if there is danger that by one group's joining the World Council of Churches the gap between them and other Mennonite groups would be greater, then that action must be carefully weighed.

In the meantime, however, there is a good deal that we can do. We can serve as a third party, a catalyst, to stimulate discussion among *all* Christians. There is evidence that the main Reformation churches today recognize value in a third position. As a third unaligned party, you can talk to both major aligned parties. Fundamentalists do not mistrust the Mennonites because they say these folks aren't in the World Council of Churches, so they are probably not too dangerous. On the other hand, the people of the World Council of Churches say they are also interested in talking with the Southern Baptists and with the Missouri Synod and with all the other smaller groups. Let us look at the possibility of the Mennonites serving for the time being, at least, as a catalyst, as a third party, which stimulates this kind of intergroup discussion. There are many levels on which this could take place, in which large segments of the church and of other disciplines or areas are simply not confronting each other, and a third party could really work as a catalyst. If somebody would say, well, this is not really Anabaptist, is it? we can refer to the disputations.

One of the greatest things that we need to do is to recover the centrality of the Great Commission. This would be, then, to move from the church scene to the pagan scene, and there is a pagan scene. There is a paganism at the heart of much of American life, which is, I'm sure, as deep as the paganism which Abraham discovered at Shechem or Paul discovered at Athens or anywhere else he may have gone. To speak thus sometimes makes us uneasy because we say, who are we to say those are the people that need the gospel? That takes an awful lot of audacity. The interesting thing is that some of the people in the psychological sciences who have had so much fun analyzing people who are driven by some kind of compulsion, these same people have been the most effective in communicating their own tremendous sense of mission.

Freud borders on megalomania in that he thinks every single problem can be solved by psychoanalysis. Every teacher, he felt, ought to be psychoanalyzed. This is not characteristic certainly of the whole movement but ask a psychologist what kind of problem is not in his domain, and what kind of person couldn't he help.

There are people who are driven by a mission, and for the church to feel that there's a tremendous mission that it has to accomplish is not a sign of mental unbalance. In our recovery of mission, we will consider ourselves as a third party, and as a winning group again. To these two we ought to join the solid conviction of being consistent apostles of a noncoercive way of dealing with hostility. Gregory Zilboorg, a famous psychiatrist, in one of his books says that the term we use, "hostility," is simply a quasi-respectable term for hatred, and it is. But if this is so, then the tensions that in varying degrees are felt to exist between the church and psychiatry would dissolve quickly. Certainly, most enlightened psychiatry today will not say that a human being who is mentally ill should be given a shock of electricity as *we* do our cattle when *we* want them on the truck. There is a noncoercive way of dealing with mental illness which we should have no difficulty espousing. When a couple confronts divorce and wants to express their hostility toward each other in this terrible radical break, it's one thing for the church to say, you do that and you'll be damned—you're going to hell. It's quite another for us to say: "Look at what will happen to your children and look at what will happen to you if you do this." Then in a noncoercive way seek to help and to resolve this hostility, and it's been done often. At the heart, then, it seems to me there's a very close affinity here to what we have always believed.

Summary

We began by looking at the essence of Anabaptism and concluded that the power of the resurrected Christ and the new life in Christ constitutes that essence. Resurrection power, freedom of sonship, and joy to live the Christian life permeate the early Anabaptist writings. Alongside this new power to live the life in Christ was also a radical new loyalty to him which puts all other loyalties into perspective. The state and the family and other human institutions were not slighted but their demands were met only through Christ. As part of this new power there was the strong conviction that the power of love could triumph over all hostility and evil. They also believed that Christians are different, and that because of this difference they should continue to be winning those outside of Christ. All of these basic insights were felt to retain their relevance and it would seem that my slackening of efforts in speaking to the church and to the world would be inconsistent with the Anabaptist heritage.

5

Radical Reformation[1]

Introduction

WALTER KLAASSEN

In this series of studies I have abandoned the well-established and legitimate division usually used in this segment of the seminar in order to focus, in slightly different fashion, on some aspects of our historical tradition that appear to me to be of special importance for the contemporary church scene and therefore for us.

It would, however, be unwise to take the titles too seriously, since they are designed to be pointers, general indicators, rather than precise descriptions. I also confess to yielding to the temptation of sensationalism, of bandwagonism, in my selection of topics. It will be up to the reader to determine whether they have any merit.

In connection with that, a word about the term "radical." The word, as we all know, is built from "*radix*," Latin for "root." Contrary to some popular assumption we should recognize that the word "radical" does not carry a uniform, unchanging freight of meaning. It is a purely relative term, for we must always ask, "Radical with reference to what?" What was once considered radical, such as the political view known as liberalism, has now

---

1. The introduction to the first of five lectures published here, originally presented to a Student Services Summer Seminar, Elkhart, IN, August 1964.

become commonplace and is in some circles equated with the status quo. What appears radical to one person may appear reactionary to another. The word "radical" has been used adjectivally of Anabaptism because in its reform of the church it went consciously and deliberately to primitive models for guidance. Its cry was "Back to the Sources!"—the assumption being that what had happened between 325 and 1525 was mostly in error. In that historical sense, then, the Anabaptists were radical. But it goes deeper than that. They were radical not simply because they were more biblicistic, but because through really listening to the Bible they developed thoroughgoing, radical, to-the-roots criticism of some basic religious assumptions of the times. In that sense also they were radical, and when I use the term, I use it with both of these connotations. I will also allow it to carry some of the color the word has acquired in our contemporary culture. Some of the adjectives are: dangerous, revolutionary, destructive, irresponsible, undependable, and immoral. For these very words were used of our sixteenth-century fathers by the representatives of established orders in church and state.

One more introductory note. The sources I have selected for inclusion come from virtually all segments of early Anabaptism. But they are limited. Nor do the spokesmen always speak for all Anabaptists. Sometimes they represent a minority position, and their views ought therefore not to be attributed to the whole movement. Nevertheless, they do represent the movement, inasmuch as their authors were Anabaptists. They attest to the variety and richness of the tradition, as well as to the various levels of human ability among the writers.

In these studies, I shall try to discuss what was. You need not assume that because I say it, I accept it just as they did.

Although I describe here the Anabaptist position and one with which I identify myself, I do not want to be read as taking the view that everyone else in the sixteenth century must have been either morally or mentally retarded. Other positions also have an inner coherence and logic. But here we are concerned about Anabaptism.

5.1

Radical Reformation 1

Radical Religion: Anabaptism and the Sacred

Walter Klaassen

Perhaps the most "radical" of all Anabaptist documents is the one referred to by the late Fritz Blanke as the earliest document of the free church, the letter of Conrad Grebel and his friends to Thomas Müntzer, the Lutheran preacher turned radical reformer.[1] It was written in September 1524, some four months before the actual birth of the new community, in the hope of gaining open and sympathetic support from one whom they considered to be near to their own interests and convictions.

It seems accurate to refer to this document as the charter of the free church. But surely it goes much deeper than that, for it testifies to the rejection not only of priestly and magisterial absolutism; it attacks the basis on which those two were able to develop. It is, if you like, the charter for the renewal of biblical religion. The emphasis of pages seventy-six to seventy-eight reveals nothing so much as a repeated and careful reading of the words of Jesus in the Gospels, Paul's words about the law, and the words of the Old Testament prophets about religious observances and ceremonies and the divine demands for justice and love and mercy. It is the old question already

---

1. Williams and Mergal, *Spiritual and Anabaptist*, 73–85.

asked centuries before Christ as to what constitutes the holiness which God is and demands of men. And to this question they gave, in my estimation, the biblical answer.

It is the uniform testimony of Anabaptism that sacredness or holiness does not belong to special persons, objects, days, words, and places. We will allow Grebel's letter to serve as the representative example. In this they rejected centuries-long Christian and an even longer pre- and para-Christian understanding of the sacred, a tradition which even today has a strong hold on Western Christianity. We begin with point ten on page seventy-six:[2] "The Supper of fellowship Christ did institute and plant," and in point eleven we are already on the *words*. Words are used with the Supper, but in the first place only the words from the Gospels or 1 Corinthians are to be said. Secondly, since in the old church the words from the Gospels are also used, the letter clarifies their function. They are words of institution, not of consecration. Grebel and his friends had grown up with the Mass in which when the priest intoned the words, "*Hoc est corpus meum* [This is my own body]," the bread and the wine were transubstantiated into the body and blood of Jesus. The function of the words was consecrational; in fact, they had a magical function. From this they wanted to dissociate themselves completely. Hence the insistence on the nonsacred function of the words; they are simply the legitimation for the observance of the Supper.

There are no sacred *things*. "The bread is nothing but bread," they emphasize in point sixteen, and therefore ordinary bread ought to be used, and it should be treated like ordinary bread. Again, the practice of the old church prompted their emphasis. Special bread was prepared for the Mass, which was sanctified by the priest before use. Moreover, the priest drank the wine from a specially sanctified cup. Now they say, "An ordinary drinking vessel too ought to be used."

There is no holy *place*. For the Supper, they write, "is not to be used in 'temples.'" Why not? To this point I let Peter Rideman, a Hutterite leader, speak. He wrote this in 1542:

> With regard to the building of stone and wood—these originated, as the history of several showeth, when this country was forced by the sword to make a verbal confession of the Christian faith. Further, men dedicated temples to their gods, and then made them "Churches," as they are wrongly named, of the Christians. Thus, they originated through the instigation of the devil and are built

2. Williams and Mergal, *Spiritual and Anabaptist*, 76.

> up through sacrifice to the devils.... For that is also not God's will, for Christ hath no fellowship with Belial. Therefore, also, hath he commanded in the Old Testament that they should utterly destroy and break down such places, that they might not share in that fellowship. No where doth he say, change it and use it aright; but saith break it down utterly.
>
> Now, because the people did this not, but left the root in the earth, they not only brought not the heathen practices to the right usage, but they themselves forsook the right usage and surrendered themselves to all manner of idolatry, and they have now changed so much that they call "saints" what those called "gods." And for the same reason because the root is left in the earth—they have gone farther and have built one house after another for their gods (or "saints" as they call them), and filled them with their gods and idols, and thereby show that they are the children of their fathers and have not left their fellowship.[3]

Although there is no positive statement in the letter, we know that in subsequent practice they joined in the Supper in their homes. Doing it in church creates a false reverence, as though it has more validity there than elsewhere. Point twenty-two says that "it should be used much and often." This may seem to be an intensification of concern for religious action. However, it should be seen in the context of the canon from the Fourth Lateran Council of 1215 which stated that every believer should commune at least once a year. The simple act of communion once a year was deemed a minimum, but adequate, sanctification for the believer. It should be used often, they write in point twenty, precisely because it is "not a Mass and sacrament."

Again there is no special sacred *person*. "A server from out of the congregation" should pronounce the words. Moreover, it should be served "without priestly garment and vestment." But actually, they write to Müntzer, "it ought not to be administered by thee. That was the beginning of the Mass that only a few would partake." The fact, of course, was that the wine was considered so precious that no layman was allowed to have it, for fear it would be spilled. Therefore, only the specially consecrated person, the priest, drank it. The concern of Grebel and his friends is that this practice of isolating one person as more sacred than another be abandoned. Hence they say, "therefore none is to receive it alone."[4] The rejection of the notion

---

3. Rideman, *Confession*, 94–95.
4. Williams and Mergal, *Spiritual and Anabaptist*, 76–77.

of the sacredness of some persons as over against others is also expressed by Michael Sattler in his last defense. It is dealt with in point five in which he says that no one is any more sacred than anyone else. All who belong to Christ are saints, and those who have gone to be with Christ he refers to by distinction, as "the blessed."[5] The sum of the matter is that any person agreed upon by the congregation handles the bread and the wine because since he has faith in Christ he is a saint.[6] Sattler enlarges on this in his reply to the seventh charge against him. He was charged with having broken his monastic vow of chastity. It was assumed that a monk, like a cleric, was especially sanctified, and to enter the state of marriage was to compromise his sanctity, grounded partly in asceticism. He rejects the idea that to marry makes a man unclean or unfit to serve God, or that in marrying a man has offended against the holiness which he demands of his servants.[7]

Finally, they rejected the sacredness of *time*. Grebel and his friends make no direct reference to it (unless point twenty-five speaks to the subject), but another notable Anabaptist does. There is a reflection of Pilgram Marpeck on the observance of the Sabbath (presumably Sunday), written to the Swiss Brethren in 1531. The Swiss Brethren were inclined to insist on abstention from all physical work on Sunday. Marpeck argues that Christ has set us free from the tyranny of time.

> Whoever today does not keep the Sabbath in Jesus Christ the Son of God, that is, whoever does no work, stands idle, and in all of his life even to death *seeks himself in work for himself,* he breaks the Sabbath. For the Son of God has established the celebration and the obedience to death, yes the death on the cross, for all flesh and blood. For whoever seeks himself will find death and whoever loses his life finds life. This is the Sabbath which the children of God observe and of which they are lords with Christ. For their flesh and blood with its lusts must celebrate in Christ into death with its sinful works. This is not a reference to physical work necessary for life otherwise we could not eat, drink, or clothe ourselves.
>
> However, the bodily celebration of the Sabbath can be good, provided it is done in freedom of the spirit and not bound to time, state, and person by a law. Otherwise it is not a celebration for God and the neighbor in love which is the true celebration. Rather one accepts the tyranny of time which has already been fulfilled by

---

5. Williams and Mergal, *Spiritual and Anabaptist*, 140.
6. See also Wenger, "Schleitheim Confession," art. 5, 250.
7. Williams and Mergal, *Spiritual and Anabaptist*, 140.

Jesus Christ, and means that we should now rule over time. If we bind it to the state we cause the kingdom of earth to rule over man when in fact he is lord of the whole earth with Christ in patience.[8]

In the same passage a little further along he also argues for the discontinuance of saints' days. They are not special days just because they are bound to a special person. If one is compelled to observe special days, he writes, "one accepts the tyranny of time which has already been fulfilled by Jesus Christ, and which means that we should now rule over time." The general point made here can be substantiated over and over again from other Anabaptist writings.

Several other special examples should be added. Christian faith was regarded by all Christians as a divine revelation. The medium of revelation according to Christian thinkers from the Fathers onward was the church itself. It had, therefore, come to be conceived of as spotlessly holy by virtue of the holiness of the clergy. It was also regarded as infallible by virtue of the guidance of the one Holy Spirit of God. The church was therefore described as holy in and of itself in its essence and being and visible manifestation. But Anabaptists applied a test other than that of sacramental ordination. Listen to Menno Simons:

> It is true enough that the papists teach and believe that Jesus Christ is the Son of God, that He sacrificed His flesh and shed His blood for us. But they also say that if we wish to partake thereof and share in it we must obey the pope and belong to his church, hear mass, receive the holy water, go on pilgrimages, call upon the mother of the Lord and the deceased saints, go to confessional at least twice a year, receive papistic absolution, have our children baptized, and keep the holy days and fast days in Lent. The priests must vow "chastity"; the bread in their mass must be called the flesh of Christ, and the wine the blood of Christ . . . .
>
> And all of this the poor ignorant people call the most holy Christian faith and the institution of the holy Christian church. Although actually it is nothing but human invention, self-chosen righteousness, open seduction of souls, manifest deception of the soul, an intolerable make-a-living and gain of the lazy priests, an accursed abomination, provocation of God, shameful blasphemy, an unworthy despising of the blood of Christ, invented notions, and a disobedient refusal to bow to the holy Word of God. In short, a false, offensive religion and open idolatry, things concerning

---

8. Marpeck, "Judgment and Decision," 46r–46v.

> which Jesus Christ . . . has not left nor commanded us a single letter.
>
> And this is not yet enough that they practice such abominations. But they proceed also to despise as vain and useless all the true fruits of faith, commanded by the Son of God Himself: the genuine, pure love and fear of God, the love and service of our neighbors, and the true sacraments and worship.[9]

In this passage Menno speaks like the Old Testament prophets, clearly saying that no matter how vaulting the claims of holiness, they are an abomination unless they receive expression in true love of God and man. Holiness divorced from truth and love is a deception and a lie. The institution of the Roman church, therefore, as Anabaptists saw it, was rejected as the carrier of God's revelation, since it lacked the true holiness.

Within the church as the medium of revelation was a special channel, the Bible. It occupied an honored place in Roman Christianity and was elevated by Luther into the supreme authority over against hierarchy and tradition. But for some Anabaptists the Bible too was too highly rated. They saw Protestants making a fetish out of it, making the divine salvation of man depend on one thing to the exclusion of all others. Hans Denck valued the Scriptures above all earthly treasures. But, he writes, "salvation cannot be tied to the Scriptures, however important and good they may be with respect to it. The reason is that it is not possible for the Scriptures to improve an evil heart even if it is highly learned. A pious heart, however, that is a heart in which there is a true spark of godly zeal will be improved through all things."[10] The Scriptures are unquestionably important for Denck, as he discusses elsewhere, but they are always only a material witness to the Word of God which is ultimately not tied to things. For this reason he says that a person with the right spirit will be improved not only by the Bible, but by *all* things. The Scriptures are therefore not uniquely holy or sacred, although they do serve a special function. It should be said here that, although there is support for this view of the Scriptures from elsewhere in the Anabaptist tradition, it was not uniformly held.

Of the whole question one can say that the Anabaptists rejected totally the notion of *ex opere operato* in its Roman and Protestant forms and were ready to take the consequences of such a radical position. Did they then deny the reality of holiness or sacredness altogether? I do not believe so.

---

9. Simons, *Complete Writings*, 332–33.
10. Denck, *Shriften II*, 160.

They frequently speak of holiness but in its basic biblical sense which is personal and ethical in nature. This means also that the observance of baptism and the Supper, upon which they insisted with the authority of Jesus, had significance in terms, not of the rites themselves, but of their function in the community. Baptism signifies a changed life in virtue of Christ's death but by no means in an individualistic sense. Repeatedly they insist that no one is "to be baptized without Christ's rule of binding and loosing" (Matt 18:15–22). That means basically that the one baptized commits himself to the discipline of the community. He thereby declares himself ready to participate in dealing with sin in the community in a new and redemptive way. He not only commits himself to live the new life in obedience to the words of Christ, but he also agrees to receive and to give active, deliberate help in doing so. The Supper is described from the beginning as "the supper of fellowship." It has nothing to do with "external reverence" (perhaps the feeling or mood of worship?) nor with "veneration of the bread" or "adoration" of the wine. The "true understanding and appreciation of the supper" is that it is "the incorporation with Christ and the brethren." "Although it is simply bread, yet if faith and brotherly love precede it, it is to be received with joy, since, when it is used in the church, it is to show us that we are truly one bread and one body, and that we are and wish to be true brethren with one another." Further, it is a commitment of willingness "to live and suffer for the sake of Christ and the brethren, of the head and members."[11] God wants all men to live together in harmony. Ulrich Stadler in his *Cherished Instruction* says that the ordinances of Christ "should constitute the polity for the whole world."[12] Since, however, not everyone will follow Christ, those who do form the community which God desires and live according to his will in mutual truth, love, and aid. They conceive of themselves, therefore, not as another cultic community but as the community of those who deliberately resolve to realize in the present God's will for the whole of mankind. Peter Rideman writes about the church:

> The Church of Christ is the basis and ground of truth, a lantern of righteousness, in which the light of grace is borne and held before the whole world, that its darkness, unbelief and blindness be thereby seen and made light, and that men may also learn to see and know the way of life. Therefore is the Church of Christ in the first place completely filled with the light of Christ as a lantern

---

11. Williams and Mergal, *Spiritual and Anabaptist*, 76.
12. Williams and Mergal, *Spiritual and Anabaptist*, 278.

is illuminated and made bright by the light, that His light might shine through her to others.[13]

A community that does this is holy because it is united with God in his will and purpose in and through Jesus Christ.

This is the heart of what I call the radical religion of Anabaptism: a return to the biblical understanding of the sacred. This is not to say that there were no others who even in their time had grasped their understanding of things. There is a measure of it in Protestantism as well as in Roman Christianity. But they were the only ones who sought to find and express God's will in radically personal and communal terms. The meaning of "radically" in this last sentence I hope to show in subsequent studies.

---

13. Rideman, *Confession*, 39–40.

5.2

Radical Reformation 2

Radical Discipleship: Anabaptism and Ethics

WALTER KLAASSEN

This study is really a continuation of the first in that it deals in more detail with the content of the notion of holiness or the sacred in Anabaptism. For Anabaptists, as for all other Christians in the sixteenth century, Christian faith was a revealed faith. God was the Author of it, and the Mediator of it was Jesus Christ. When Hans Denck refused to call the Bible the Word of God, he did so only because he reserved the title for Jesus himself. "Jesus Christ is the Word of God" we hear again and again from all segments of Anabaptism. It is the human Jesus about whom they speak, God revealed in the man of flesh and blood. Pilgram Marpeck argued that we have to begin with the humanness of Jesus if we are going to penetrate into God's intentions.

Thus, the Gospels with their accounts of Jesus's words, actions, teaching, and death become very important. By his death, which was an expression of the love and mercy of God, sin is removed, man is forgiven, and enters upon eternal life together with Christ. This has nothing to do with man's own merit, for there is none before God. It is a gift of God's grace. This is said often and explicitly enough for there to be no doubt about it. Jesus Christ is the Savior of men.

But to accept him as the Savior is only the beginning of faith. For the Jesus that died also rose again and was for his obedience made Lord by God. God's authority is embodied in him. It is to him that God bids men listen. There is no other authority for men except this one, for their eternal destiny depends upon how they relate to him. Thus, it is not only dependence upon the shed blood of Christ that constitutes "listening to him." In his work *The New Birth* Menno Simons touches on this point:

> Some may answer: Our belief is that Christ is the Son of God, that His word is truth, and that He purchased us with His blood and truth. We were regenerated in baptism and we received the Holy Ghost; therefore, we are the true church and congregation of Christ.
>
> We reply: If your faith is as you say, why do you not do the things which He has commanded you in His Word? . . . Since you do not do as He commands and desires, but as you please, it is sufficiently proved that you do not believe that Jesus Christ is the Son of God, although you say so.[1]

Obedience to Christ the Lord is an integral part of faith. In Hans Denck's first public statement he says this about faith:

> Faith is the obedience to God and the confidence in His promise through Jesus Christ. Where this obedience is absent there all confidence is false and a deception. This obedience must be genuine, that is, that heart, mouth, and deed coincide together. For there can be no true heart where neither mouth nor deed is visible.[2]

Faith then is confidence in the certainty of God's love and grace as shown in Jesus and following him, which is the evidence that the confidence is genuine. Christ is the Lord not only in that salvation is through him alone, but also in that he becomes the One Who determines what a man is and does as the model and example of a God-pleasing life. "The true evangelical faith," writes Menno elsewhere, "sees and considers only the doctrine, ceremonies, commands, prohibitions, and the perfect example of Christ, and strives to conform thereto with all its power."[3] And again: "Let Christ Jesus with His Spirit and Word be your teacher and example, your way and your mirror."[4] Or, "Whosoever boasts that he is a Christian, the

1. Simons, *Complete Writings*, 96.
2. Denck, *Shriften II*, 107.
3. Simons, *Complete Writings*, 343.
4. Simons, *Complete Writings*, 96.

same must walk as Christ walked."[5] There is a call here and in thousands of other passages in Anabaptist writings, for a very concrete following of the example of Christ. In fact, it is in this following of Christ that truth is to be found. Hans Hut writes in his *The Mystery of Baptism*:

> No one can attain to the truth unless he follows in the footsteps of Christ and His elect in the school of tribulation. At the very least he must have declared that he will follow Him in the will of God in the justification of Christ's cross. For no one can learn the mysteries of divine wisdom in the den of murderers' cave of all knavery, as they think in Wittenberg or Paris.[6]

Truth is therefore not abstract and ideological but existential in nature. It is not discovered in Paris, the seat of medieval Catholic learning, nor in Wittenberg, the new Lutheran seat of learning. Rather, it is discovered in the footsteps of Christ in everyday life. Thus, the learned are not in the universities, courts, or seats of the church hierarchies. Rather, says Hut, "Look to the poor, those who are despised by the world and called visionaries, and devils according to the example of Christ and the apostles.[7]

Discipleship is expressed in the disciple's relationship to others, both outside as well as inside the church. A disciple's relationships are governed by love and truth, even as Christ's were. And the command to love and truth is unconditional. No condition of religion or society, of church or state, in any way qualifies these demands. It was one of the complaints of Grebel and many another Anabaptist that men modified the demands of the Lord Jesus to suit the prevailing religious and social conditions. "We too," he writes, "are thus rejected by our learned shepherds. All men follow them, because they preach a sinful sweet Christ,"[8] a Christ that made little or no demands of his followers. They neglect to tell men about the "bitter Christ," in Hans Hut's words, that is, about the uncompromising difficulty of his demands.

And indeed, their understanding of Christ's demands frequently conflicted with the demands of the religious and social order of the time. They espoused the cause of religious liberty which crossed the accepted views and methods of church discipline. For it was assumed by Catholic and Protestant alike that dissenters had to be dealt with by force if they did not yield

---

5. Simons, *Complete Writings*, 225.
6. Hut, "Mystery of Baptism," 82.
7. Hut, "Mystery of Baptism," 81.
8. Williams and Mergal, *Spiritual and Anabaptist*, 78–79.

to other persuasion. This is the point of Grebel's comment that "such a man [one persisting in disobedience], we say, taught by God's Word, shall not be killed, but regarded as a heathen and publican and let alone."[9] Whatever we may think about regarding a man as a heathen and publican, the point is that when persuasion by God's word failed he ought to be allowed to hold his error without losing his head. With some individual exceptions this was regarded by all in sixteenth-century Europe as an invitation to anarchy and therefore quite intolerable.

To the Anabaptists, however, it was consistent with their Lord's command to love all men and with their conviction that God's truth needed no human coercion to be victorious. Menno Simons's words to those Anabaptists who advocated violence actually also typify the general Anabaptist position: "If he [the Christian] is to instruct in meekness those that oppose truth, how can he angrily punish them that do not as yet acknowledge the truth?"[10] They held to their position even though they themselves were persecuted.

Their refusal to participate in warfare also brought them nothing but trouble. Fighting and killing was contrary to the law of love, no matter how much the situation might seem to demand it. Such people could not be trusted since they would not agree to defend the established order. The same thing held for their refusal to pay taxes for military purposes.[11] Their refusal to swear oaths was not only an expression of concern for truthfulness. Many of them found themselves faced with swearing an oath of allegiance to the state of which they were citizens. Such an oath involved the commitment to bear arms on behalf of that state and in its defense. It was an oath they could not take and therefore they often found themselves deprived of their citizenship. Most frequently the penalty was exile which involved the loss of home, property and position.

Again their discipleship led them into a new attitude towards property. When a person entered the community, he put all that he had at the disposal of the brothers. While this did not necessarily involve a common treasury, it did mean that no Christian could call his property his own as though it had nothing to do with others. In 1528 a group of Anabaptists moved to a common treasury under pressure of external circumstances.

---

9. Williams and Mergal, *Spiritual and Anabaptist*, 79–80.
10. Simons, *Complete Writings*, 46.
11. Rideman, *Confession*, 109–11.

Ulrich Stadler writes about property as being closely related to man's selfishness.[12] This was radical on both the individual and social levels. Those in positions of political and economic power were very afraid of this, for if it ever became widespread, they would be the ones to lose.

Their unhesitating refusal to obey the governments in matters relating to faith and the church got them the reputation of being rebels. When Conrad Grebel and others refused to have their infants baptized by order of the City Council in Zurich in January 1525, they were given an ultimatum: either get your children baptized or get out. When Anabaptist citizens of Bern in 1538 would not abandon their views, they were sent into exile with the threat that if ever they returned their lives would be forfeited. Felix Manz, one of the early leaders, suffered death by drowning because he refused to obey an ancient ordinance that prohibited rebaptism.

Elsewhere they were in danger just because of their exemplary lives. If a man did not drink to excess, curse, abuse his workmen or family, he could be suspected of being an Anabaptist and thus subject to prosecution. *An Introduction to Mennonite History*, edited by C. J. Dyck, cites an example:

> Because he does not swear and because he leads an inoffensive life, therefore men suspect [Hans Jeger] of Anabaptism.... He has for a long time passed for such because he did not swear, nor quarrel, nor did other such-like things.[13]

The refusal to participate in Catholic or Protestant worship and the Mass or Lord's Supper also rendered them subject to persecution. And most of all, their insistence on forming their own community was regarded as a grave offense since according to accepted understanding it produced schism in the church and a rupture in the general social structure.

It was their seriousness about conforming with all their power to the perfect example of Christ that brought them into conflict with the prevailing order at so many points. It was a radical, uncompromising discipleship which they espoused.

But while their discipleship had about it an existential quality, it should not be confused with an individualistic, fatalistic, stoic, lonely, jump-in-the-dark type of existentialism that still enjoys some popularity. While the decision to become a disciple was an individual step of faith, the new life upon which the disciple entered was communal. Becoming a disciple did

---

12. Williams and Mergal, *Spiritual and Anabaptist*, 278–79.
13. Dyck, *Introduction*, 312.

not isolate him; it brought him for the first time into a true community in which he could find himself, and in which he could get resources and help on the incredibly steep and narrow way he had chosen to go. This is clearly indicated in Leopold Scharnschlager's little church order of 1540:

> Since manifold deceptions are gaining ground every where it is necessary that the called, surrendered, and obligated members of Jesus Christ, wherever they are in the world and in distress, should, insofar as it is possible for them, not abandon their gatherings. Rather when and however they can according to opportunity of places and persecutions, they come together for the sake of the love of Christ. . . . This must take place in wisdom, moderation, good sense, discipline, friendliness, and a quiet manner. This is all the more important since we see that the day of the Lord is near.[14]

Life in the community is necessary in order not to lose hold on the truth. It is not axiomatic that one will remain true since the world is full of deception. Deception is the norm and on the increase. The distress of persecution and the strain under which that puts a Christian is a cogent reason for not neglecting the close association with others of like commitment. The danger of being deceived and the reality of persecution make it imperative that one knows what is important and basic.

But what is even more important is that the community of Jesus, the church, is that human community in which men learn to live with each other as they ought to live, "peaceably, united, lovingly, amicably, and fraternally as children of one Father."[15] The habits that are learned in the church also govern behavior and attitudes to those outside.

The purpose of the Supper, especially, is to express in signal form the reality of this new community of love and peace and truth. The letter of Grebel and his friends to Müntzer repeatedly makes reference to "the rule of Christ" or "Christ's rule of binding and loosing" found in Matt 18:15–18.

The Supper should never be used without it.[16] It is not a legal formula disclosing the steps by which a person should be expelled from the church—although it is often interpreted that way—but a way of dealing with sin and evil in the new community. This is surely one of the most radical aspects of Anabaptist discipleship for they clearly assume that the company of Jesus's disciples, that is the church, forgives and retains sin. If this community is in

---

14. Scharnschlager, "Church Order," 131.
15. Williams and Mergal, *Spiritual and Anabaptist*, 278.
16. Williams and Mergal, *Spiritual and Anabaptist*, 77.

fact to be the community of obedience—and this, writes Menno, is one of the marks of the church[17]—it must deal with disobedience. It cannot simply be left, for the nature of sin is to multiply once it springs to life. If sin occurs, the one who knows about it is responsible to get rid of it. The provision is that privacy about it be preserved. It must not become public property, so that the failure becomes the subject of gossip and ignorant judgment. And if it can be settled at that level it is done, loosing or forgiveness has taken place. It may, for one reason or another, go further, but the same rule of privacy applies for the protection of the one who sinned. Only as a last resort does separation take place, when clear incompatibility of life and conviction have been established. When that happens, the person remains bound or the sin is retained. A sin cannot be forgiven unless it is acknowledged, and forgiveness is liberation of the offender. Discipleship is therefore very much a communal matter, and that is why Grebel wrote that "even an adult is not to be baptized without Christ's rule of binding and loosing."[18] When one becomes a disciple one recognizes that he is not capable of being one by himself and that he needs the help and understanding of others to walk the steep and narrow way of life.

This insistence on the function of the community was a rejection on the one hand of authoritarian church discipline as exercised by the hierarchy in Roman and Reformed Christianity and also of the doctrine of the invisibility of the church as held by Lutheran and Reformed Christianity in which, since the church was believed to be invisible, the rule of Christ could not be applied. It was also expressive of a very high view of man and of the present working of God among men. Any person who had been caught by the spirit of Jesus and the genuineness of whose confession was clearly evident in attitudes and deeds was able to live in this new community. Since God gave the commandment to love all men, to live the truth, and to do it in a community, they straightforwardly assumed that it was possible in this world here and now, and that God would give his power and spirit to those who asked him.

Finally, it was assumed and understood that this community would be a suffering community. Jesus had said that the New Testament writings all had the shadow of persecution over them. They believed that anyone who was serious about following Christ would be persecuted simply because both church and state resisted the faithful doing of God's will, since

---

17. Simons, *Complete Writings*, 740.
18. Williams and Mergal, *Spiritual and Anabaptist*, 80.

it would bring all their proud institutional and theological towers crashing to the ground. In being the visible church, they were setting up a counter-society which, whether they intended it or not, challenged the existing one. From the point of view of the authorities this could not be tolerated, hence fierce and persistent persecution.

But the suffering of the disciple is not accidental. It belongs to being a disciple. Listen to Conrad Grebel:

> True Christian believers are as sheep among wolves, sheep for the slaughter; they must be baptized in anguish and affliction, tribulation, persecution, suffering and death. They must be tried with fire, and must reach the fatherland of eternal rest, not by killing their bodily but by mortifying their spiritual enemies.[19]

Hans Hut too spoke of the Christians' true baptism as suffering, a continuous experience of tribulation and the cross of Christ for the sake of Christ and the truth. It is necessary to learning the truth; suffering is "the school of tribulation."[20] Menno Simons spoke of suffering as a mark of the church. After quoting Matt 24:9 and 2 Tim 3:12 he quotes Sir 2:1–4:

> My son, if thou come to serve the Lord, prepare thy soul for temptation. Set thy heart aright, and constantly endure, and make not haste in time of trouble. Cleave unto Him, and depart not away, that thou mayest be increased at thy last end. Whatsoever is brought upon thee, take cheerfully, and be patient when thou art changed to a low estate. For gold is tried in the fire, and acceptable men in the furnace of adversity.

He continues:

> This very cross is a sure indicator of the church of Christ, and has been testified not only in olden times by the Scriptures, but also by the example of Jesus Christ, of the holy apostles and prophets, the first and unfalsified church, and also by the present pious, faithful children, especially in these our Netherlands.[21]

It is assumed that a disciple will be a nonconformist in the most radical sense. This too is following the example of Jesus.

Nor was it only an ideal which was held up as worthy to be aspired to. It was actually lived and thousands upon thousands endured torture,

---

19. Williams and Mergal, *Spiritual and Anabaptist*, 80.
20. Hut, "Mystery of Baptism," 93–95.
21. Simons, *Complete Writings*, 741–42.

imprisonment, exile, and death. They proved by this final test the radical nature of their discipleship. It was all or nothing. They believed Jesus when he said, "You cannot serve two masters."

5.3

Radical Reformation 3

Radical Theology: Anabaptism and Idealism

WALTER KLAASSEN

A hostile distrust of traditional and contemporary theologians' theology and theologizing runs through the writings of sixteenth-century Anabaptism. As with the Hebrew prophets, some of the harshest criticisms are leveled by the Anabaptists at the religious leaders of the people, in this case the Catholic and Protestant theologians and teachers. Certainly they had in mind the words of Jesus against the religious leaders of his day when they referred to their contemporaries as "scribes and Pharisees" with all that that implied.

The earliest instances of this hostility are found in the Grebel letter. He writes about the "evangelical preachers" who "falsely forbear and act and set their own opinions . . . above God and against God," about "the slothful scholars and doctors at Wittenberg," and that they are more likely to be persecuted "on the part of scholars than of other people." The term "learned shepherds" recurs several times. Long discussions of this are found in Menno Simons[1] and in Peter Rideman[2] and in many other places. Most

---

1. Simons, *Complete Writings*, 207–12.
2. Rideman, *Confession*, 95–97.

of the men who are thus identified are the great names of Protestantism as well as of contemporary Roman Christianity, Luther, Zwingli, Calvin, Bucer on the one side, and the pope, archbishops, bishops, and scholars in the ancient universities on the other. When we remember that many of the early Anabaptist leaders were themselves university-trained scholars as well as former Roman clergy we must ask for the reason for this hostility. An early explanation which is not adequate is that Anabaptism's university-trained men were not good enough to hold leading positions in Roman or Protestant Christianity. While one can hardly deny that possibility in individual cases, it does not hold of all of them. One needs only to mention Michael Sattler, who before he became an Anabaptist was prior of a Benedictine monastery; Balthasar Hubmaier, who was a popular preacher and theologian in Regensburg; and Hans Denck, who did scholarly work in one of the great publishing houses in Basel and was co-translator of a popular version of the Hebrew prophets. The reason lies deeper.

When the uneducated Anabaptist layman referred to the scholar and doctor and their products in unflattering and disparaging terms, the temptation to dismiss it as the age-old proletarian scorn for the egghead is close at hand. That this figured in Anabaptism, perhaps sometimes strongly so, is readily granted. And yet that too is not a sufficient explanation, especially if we take seriously their own stated reasons for their attitude. What then is the explanation? To provide one is the purpose of this study.

Again, it would be a mistake simply to take Anabaptist statements by themselves, for in isolation they sound intolerant and disparaging of scholarship. Moreover, they appear to take pride in ignorance, in simple-mindedness. But putting all these statements into their intellectual context in the sixteenth century reveals another picture. To do this necessitates first of all a brief explanation of the subtitle: Anabaptism and Idealism. It is not what it seems. The popular meaning of the term of an ideal as distinct from reality would make it more suitable as a subtitle for the previous lecture on discipleship. What is meant by idealism here could better be conveyed if we hyphenated the word to make it idea-lism, perhaps even dropping the "l." It is the old meaning of the word which describes a philosophical assumption that ideas are real in themselves without having any particular objectification. These ideas are ultimately in the mind of God, but man is able, through the capacity of reason, to think God's thoughts after him. If man thinks carefully according to the rules of logic, he can thereby discover truth. This was supremely exemplified by Thomas Aquinas in his great argument for the existence of God from the fact of motion. He begins from an observable phenomenon and then proceeds by logical deduction that God exists and what the nature of this God is. While nominalism, the movement which rejected the independent existence of ideas, was strong after Aquinas, it had been quite unable to get rid of the basic assumption which it rejected. This assumption was in fact a basic pillar in the main philosophical substructure of Christian theology from the second century onwards. It could not be abandoned, for on it rested the whole structure of Christian thought. It was this confidence in the ability of man's reason to discover truth that was still very strong in the sixteenth century. It was natural in the thought of Roman Christianity, and not quite so natural but still quite evident in Protestantism, especially of the Reformed variety.[3]

A dramatic example of this is to be found in the minutes of the debate between Anabaptists and some Zwinglian (or Reformed) clerics in 1538 in Berne, Switzerland. The argument about the legitimacy of infant baptism was finally won by the clerics to their satisfaction by the use of a syllogism which went like this:

> All who belong to God have the Holy Spirit;
> Children belong to God;
> Therefore children have the Holy Spirit.

Since the Spirit is necessary to faith, the possession of the Spirit argues that infants have faith. When therefore the New Testament says that those who have faith are to be baptized it legitimizes the baptism also of infants.[4] This bit of sophistry joined to the divine revelation in Scripture was for them an acceptable basis for the practice of infant baptism. The idealist assumption was part of the intellectual context of the time.

The Anabaptists were convinced that error is the only outcome of such procedure, for it always made possible a softening, a neutralizing of the commands of Christ. By such means, stated Balthasar Hubmaier, one could make a new Christ out of a pumpkin.[5] Such ideas were not necessarily related to the concrete facts of church life and personal discipleship and were therefore at best suspect and at worst deceptive. Thus was the whole medieval legacy of the combination of rational and revealed theology rejected.

---

3. Tillich, *Complete History,* 262.
4. Klaassen, "Bern Debate," 151.
5. Hubmaier, *Schriften,* 132.

CONCERN FOR ANABAPTIST RENEWAL

Another part of the context was Luther's theology. The Anabaptist attitude to it is typified by the words of Hans Hut: "For the teaching one hears from them is nothing else than: 'Have faith!' and goes no farther."[6] Luther was understood by many to be saying that all one could do to be saved was to have faith in the merits of Christ, that this was the only response God required of man, and that it was the only one God accepted. It appeared to the Anabaptists to be an intellectual matter, for they could see in it no visible expression. Their understanding of the church and of discipleship called for a faith that was plainly visible in attitudes and deeds. Words lend themselves too easily to misrepresentation and to making claims which go beyond actual experience. They regarded Luther's *sola fideism* as another example of learned subtlety which was popular because it made no demands on anyone.[7] While Anabaptists did not reject the New Testament's announcement of salvation through faith, they did reject what they believed to be a misleading and abstract interpretation of it.

A third aspect of the context in which we must seek to understand Anabaptist attitudes toward theologians and theology is the legalism of the old church. This is in summary fashion described by Paul Tillich:

> The Catholic system is a system of objective, quantitative, and relative relations between God and man for the sake of providing eternal happiness for man. This is the basic structure: objective, not personal; quantitative, not qualitative; relative and conditioned, not absolute. . . . It is a system of divine-human management, represented and actualized by ecclesiastical management.[8]

Menno Simons repeatedly returns to this point as for example in his *Foundation of Christian Doctrine*. "Legends, histories, fables, holy days, images, holy water, tapers, palms, confessionals, pilgrimages, masses, matins, and vespers . . . purgatory, vigils, times, bulls, offerings"; these constitute the church's demand upon the faithful as satisfaction for sin.[9] It keeps people in the bondage of uncertainty and under pressure to do constantly more of the same in order to get a gracious God. It is a system that lacks discrimination, for it places these relatively trivial matters in the place of Christ who

---

6. Hut, "Of the Mystery of Baptism," 380.

7. Compare Bonhoeffer's discussion of "cheap grace" in *The Cost of Discipleship*, 35–47.

8. Denck, *Schriften II*, 228.

9. Simons, *Complete Writings*, 165.

alone is the source of salvation. It is "an unworthy despising of the blood of Christ.[10]

Finally, the apparatus for interpreting the Bible developed in the Middle Ages constitutes a part of the context. In addition to the literal meaning three other levels of meaning were believed to be present. These others, based on the allegorical method of interpretation, often crowded out or even invalidated the literal meaning.[11] It was a system of interpretation that could justify almost any kind of theology, since it operated without any built-in controls. If a saying of Jesus, for example, conflicted with the approved position of the church in its literal sense, it could be interpreted to yield a meaning not in conflict with the church's position. This method of interpretation was still in force in the Roman church in the sixteenth century, but the Reformers had abandoned the four levels of meaning in favor of one or at the most two. Nevertheless, enough of it remained even there to call forth charges of sophistry and clever twisting of the Scriptures.[12] When therefore we read of Anabaptists rejecting interpretation they mean the fourfold interpretive structure and the application of the rules of logic to the interpretation of Scriptures. They regarded all that as an attempt to get out from under the clear command of Christ to follow him and bear the cross.

What had happened in the estimation of the Anabaptists was that by these means the simplicity and directness of the gospel had been hopelessly compromised. Misled by their teachers, people could see only a confusing puzzle where in fact everything was crystal clear. The only way out of the dark caves of sophistry and legalism and interpretation was to go beyond all of these developments to the sources; beyond the corruption of the church to the pure spring of its beginnings, the life and teachings of Jesus and the apostles. That is the luminous source and fountain of truth; everything else is secondary and must be judged by it.

They also objected to the assumption that the traditional discipline of theology was for experts only. It was the concern and preserve of an elite which none but the specially trained could enter. But with the emphasis on the church, on every member's responsibility for being able to communicate the gospel in word, there was need for a theology or an approach to theological truth and method that was accessible to even an illiterate

10. Simons, *Complete Writings*, 133.
11. See Dyck, "From Ignatius to Wyclif," 81–82.
12. See Simons, *Complete Writings*, 801, 822 for examples.

person. In fact, what we get is what is sometimes called *Gemeindetheologie*, church- or congregation-theology, one in which every person has a stake and in terms of which he can articulate his faith. That this *Gemeindetheologie* was worked out in the *Gemeinde* can be seen from the example of the Schleitheim Confession, as well as from the fairly consistent uniformity of statements from individuals under questioning.

But the influence of individual leaders is also evident, again in the case of Schleitheim. Nor was learning rejected. Menno Simons almost vehemently rejects this charge. He had written to John à Lasco: "Let us not treat of these things in subtly invented syllogisms nor with any clever sophistries, for we do not have any of these things. But let us use in our debates only the plain and unequivocal Word that cannot be twisted with glosses, nor broken with human wisdom." John à Lasco called him a deceiver and ignorant. To this Menno said:

> Understand correctly, dear reader. Learnedness and proficiency in languages I have never disdained, but have honored and coveted them from my youth. . . . I am not so bereft of my sense that I should disdain and despise the knowledge of languages whereby the precious Word of divine grace has come to us.[13]

There is a complete and utter rejection of the scholastic assumption that divine truth comes by the two means of revelation and reason, for they saw the corruption of the church as its direct consequence.

For them revelation is the source of truth, and this divine revelation is mediated by the Scriptures. It does not consist of a collection of theological ideas but comes primarily in the life and words of Jesus Christ and the apostles. It is important to emphasize again that the words of Jesus are not separated from his life and actions. His life has theological significance, for it is the model of what God wants men to be. What Jesus said about God had immediate ethical implications as was to be expected in Judaism. We find therefore in Anabaptism no disembodied theology on the one hand and an ethical system on the other. There is a thorough fusion of the two: the one is not viable without the other. It is a theology that has immediate relevance to the everyday business of living. The Anabaptists kept insisting that their position reflected the Bible in this essential matter.

The problem with scholastic theology, as well as with Luther's, they felt, was that it so quickly moved away from what God desired of men and

---

13. Simons, *Complete Writings*, 790.

into directions in which men were destroyed. Pilgram Marpeck was especially insistent that any theological claim must be christologically based, for God's revelation in Christ represents the limits of what we know. His statement on the omnipotence of God and its corollary, predestination, illustrates the point well:

> God is a God of order and not of disorder, and He has firmly united His own omnipotence to His will and order. It is not as the predestinarians and others say without any discrimination that God has the right to all salvation and damnation. [He has, certainly,] but not outside of His order and will to which His power is subordinated, otherwise one may claim His divine power on behalf of all, as indeed Satan and his prophets are doing. Wherever the omnipotence and might of God serves their purposes they imperiously use it indiscriminately without the will of His [Jesus Christ's] Father, as Luther does with the sacrament, child baptism, infant faith, and the like. Wherever they find themselves at their wits' end they [save their theology by] appealing to the omnipotence of God.
>
> There is no sharper nor more deceitful article of false teaching than to use and preach the power and omnipotence of God outside of the order of God's Word. Further, it is the greatest blasphemy against God and the word of His truth by which He has ordered all things in heaven and on earth, in which order they shall in eternity remain. For God Himself is the wisest order in and through His Word, that is Jesus Christ His only begotten from eternity. Whoever manipulates the omnipotence of God outside of this order is a deceiver and seducer.[14]

He charges others with dabbling in things unknown which can only lead to a distortion of what we do know since it proceeds not from revelation but from reason. Marpeck also implicitly admits that our theological knowledge is always fragmentary and that the attempt to fill the gaps ought to be abandoned as dangerous.

Their treatment of the practice of infant baptism and the reason for it, namely, the doctrine of original sin, is a good example of how they came to reject traditional positions. They saw infant baptism as a practical inference from the doctrine of original sin, which had no support in Scripture. Sin, they argue, came into the world with the awakening of the knowledge of good and evil according to Gen 3. An infant does not have this knowledge

---

14. Marpeck, "Judgment and Decision," 47v–48r.

and therefore has no sin. Consequently it needs no baptism for the removal of sin. Statements by Marpeck and Grebel illustrate this position:

> When we baptize the children we throw them into damnation and death together with sinners and unbelieving deceit contrary to the blessings of Christ. For children have no sin, faith, or unbelief and can therefore confess none. For baptism witnesses to death under sin and unbelief into which we have come and in which we lie, and that it all be crucified with Christ and buried in His death. For in that we have died we have died to sin, in order that we may live in Christ in whom is forgiveness of sin and the promise of eternal life. But this has already been promised to children. . . . When the children grow in the knowledge of good and evil, in carnal reason and the cunning of the serpent which is enmity against God, only then do sin, death, and condemnation come into play. . . . Since the guilt of sin exists in the knowledge of sin, Christ has taken away the sin of the world by His blood, the innocent through the word of promise, the guilty through faith in Him. Although innocence contains a root of sin in the manner of flesh, it is still not sin itself.[15]

> All children who have not yet come to the discernment of the knowledge of good and evil, and have not yet eaten of the tree of knowledge, that they are merely saved by the suffering of Christ, the new Adam, who has restored their vitiated life, because they would have been subject to death and condemnation only if Christ had not suffered; but they're not yet grown up to the infirmity of our broken nature—unless, indeed, it can be proved that Christ did not suffer for children. But as to the objection that faith is demanded of all who are to be saved, we exclude children from this and hold that they are saved without faith, and we do not believe from the above passages [that children must be baptized].[16]

Moreover a child cannot agree to be subject to the rule of Christ without which no one may be baptized.

The idea of the omnipotence of God therefore has no value except as it relates to Christ. Similarly the doctrine of original sin is seen as a denial of the grace of God in Christ. The test of a theological statement therefore was always the life and doctrine of Christ and the apostles. By this they also established levels of authority within the Bible; they did not take a uniform view of it as though all parts were of equal significance. They rejected as

---

15. Krebs and Rott, *Elsass 1*, 459–61.
16. Williams and Mergal, *Spiritual and Anabaptist*, 81.

God's word whatever did not agree with the life and doctrine of Christ, even though it be in the Bible.

The core of the matter, as has already been pointed out, was the fusion of theology and ethics. Truth is found in living, not in abstract reasoning. An example of their concern for the tie-in between theology and life can be seen by comparing their view of the Lord's Supper with the two Protestant views. Luther took Jesus's word, "This is my body," literally as meaning actually the body of Jesus. Then he resorted to the concept of the ubiquity of the body of Christ, a totally abstract notion to justify his literalism. Therefore the individual receives the body of Christ and so is comforted and strengthened. Calvinism took a symbolic view of the statement of Jesus, insisting that the "is" means "signifies." The Supper was a memorial act, remembering the death of Christ for man. In Anabaptism the memorial aspect is not absent but the center of gravity has shifted from the individualistic approach to the corporate. Its significance is that it signifies the oneness and unity of the church, and participation in it is a pledge of peace and a commitment to each other. It is thus very intimately related to the life of the community. Again there is the insistence that the Supper should not be used without Christ's rule of binding and loosing.

But there is a still closer bond between theology and ethics. Anabaptists often quoted Jesus's words: "Not everyone who says to me 'Lord, Lord,' shall enter the kingdom of heaven, but he who does the will of my father." If someone says, "Lord, Lord," but does not do the will of God, they say again and again, one may assume that his doctrine is false. A theology that produces an evil life cannot be true. Menno Simons discusses this at length in his *Foundation of Christian Doctrine* under the headings, "The doctrine of the preachers" and "The conduct of the preachers."[17] Their teachings are rejected because of the unregenerate lives they live and their unregenerate lives are the consequence of false doctrine. Especially their violence is evidence that they do not speak truth. Peter Rideman writes:

> That they preach not the gospel but only the literal word is shown by their own deeds, in that they drive and press men to hear their teaching by means of stocks, the dungeon and keep, torture, banishment and death.[18]

---

17. Simons, *Complete Writings*, 164–77.
18. Rideman, *Confession*, 94.

Not only does their doctrine not bear good fruit in their own lives. It is because of their perversion of the gospel that things are so intolerably bad in their church. Listen to Menno:

> Observe what fruits and profits your office and service brings forth. For what is your doctrine but a vain and impotent sowing of wind which has neither spirit nor power? Your sacraments are an encouragement to the impenitent and your lives examples of wickedness. Where are the greedy whom you have made liberal, the drunkards whom you have made temperate, the impure you have made chaste, the proud whom you have humbled? How will you teach others, being yourselves untaught, and beget unto Christ a well-pleasing church? . . . For with you we do not find contrite hearts, true knowledge of Christ, true love, an earnest desire after the Kingdom of God, dying to earthly things, true humility, righteousness, friendliness, mercy, chastity, obedience, wisdom, truth, and peace. But everywhere we find hatred, envy, hard and cruel hearts, a loathing aversion and disdain for the divine Word, love and desire of this world, haughtiness, pride, pomp, lies, trickery, shame, adultery, fornication, robbery, burning, slaying, cursing, and all manner of wickedness.[19]

But while, in Menno's words, "words without actions do not edify," they did not therefore reject theology, not even traditional theology. Often when they were asked about their belief, they simply repeated the Apostolic Creed. They did plenty of writing themselves in defense of their position and some for their own edification. Thus they did not reject theology or theologizing or theologians, but they refused them all exemption from obedience to Christ and the path of discipleship. For only there does true learning take place. "No one can know Christ unless he follow Him in his life," wrote Hans Denck. There is no genuine apprehension of truth except in the school of Christ which is the life of discipleship. There God constantly reveals himself through the Spirit to learned and unlearned alike. The measure of understanding is not relative to the level of intellectual ability but to the measure of openness, of abandonment to God and his will.

The radicalness of this position is not defended by the Anabaptists, but it is clearly revealed in the unrelenting attempts to suppress it. It called into question much that was universally accepted, and therefore produced uncertainty and instability in the total fabric of society. This will be illustrated more specifically in study number five.

---

19. Simons, *Complete Writings*, 209.

5.4

Radical Reformation 4

Radical Freedom: Anabaptism and Legalism

Walter Klaassen

One of the chief criticisms against Anabaptism has always been that it was legalistic in nature. Luther was sure that it was nothing but a revival of monasticism with its legalistic approach to salvation. Law and gospel were basic categories of his thought. His agony in attempting to get a gracious God through "monkery," as he said, with its prayers, vigils, asceticisms, and works, and his shattering experience of salvation through grace by faith made him ever afterward very sensitive to any sign of anything that diminished the glory of God. When the Anabaptists criticized his, as they thought, one-sided *sola fideism* and emphasized that faith is visible and genuine only if expressed in action, he saw nothing but a new works-righteousness. These were the people who had submitted again to the law and therefore, according to Paul in Galatians, had no part in Christ. The same kind of charges were made against the Anabaptists by most of the Reformers and their successors. One still finds it in textbooks of church history.

The Anabaptists were very sensitive to this charge and regularly rejected it. Two statements by Menno Simons illustrate that they regarded the charges as false and slanderous:

> Because we teach from the mouth of the Lord that if we would enter into life, we must keep the commandments; that in Christ, neither circumcision nor uncircumcision avails anything but the keeping of the commandments of God; and that the love of God is that we keep His commandments, and His commandments are not grievous; therefore, the preachers have to call us heaven-stormers and merit-men, saying that we want to be saved by our own merits even though we have always confessed, and by the grace of God ever will, that we cannot be saved by means of anything in heaven or on earth other than by the merits, intercession, death, and blood of Christ.[1]

In another place he writes about the immoral living of so called Christians. He continues:

> If someone steps up in true and sincere love to admonish or reprove them for this, and point them to Christ Jesus rightly, to His doctrine, sacraments, and unblameable example, and to show that it is not right for a Christian so to boast and drink, revile and curse; then he must hear from that hour that he is one who believes in salvation by good works, is a heaven-stormer, a sectarian agitator, a rabble rouser, a make-believe Christian, a disdainer of the sacraments, or an Anabaptist![2]

Because of the consciousness of this charge, Anabaptist writings are full of statements insisting that they, like the other Reformers, hold to and teach salvation by grace through faith. Dirk Phillips, co-worker of Menno Simons, wrote:

> This is the true gospel, the pure doctrine of our God, full of grace and mercy, full of comfort, salvation, and eternal life, given to us by God from grace without our merits and works of the law, for the sake of the only eternal and precious Savior Jesus Christ.[3]

That is representative of hundreds of similar statements which are in no essential different from Luther, Calvin, or other Reformers on the same topic.

---

1. Simons, *Complete Writings*, 569.
2. Simons, *Complete Writings*, 334.
3. Williams and Mergal, *Spiritual and Anabaptist*, 236.

What then was the problem? From the Lutheran side at least it was simply the reverse side of the difficulty the Anabaptists had with Luther's *sola fidei*. Luther emphasized salvation by grace through faith alone. He did not discount good works, but rather insisted that they will follow faith even as the good tree bears good fruit. But some of Luther's statements convinced them that he was not serious about a Christlike life. When he said, "Sin bravely," what were theologically uninitiated people to think? In their estimation it cancelled out his call for a good life. In reverse, while Luther and others undoubtedly heard Anabaptist assurances of an evangelical position as documented above, they were in turn cancelled out by their constant references to "the new law," the "law of Christ," etc. Now law was for Luther the opposite of gospel and there could be no joining of the two. Any attempt at compromise was a sellout to legalism.

Again we must try to see the Anabaptist position within the context of the religious scene of the time. For while they based themselves on the Bible in their emphasis on doing God's will, the shape of their articulation of it was determined in considerable measure by other positions on the question.

The most obvious fact was the antinomian trend in the ethics of Protestantism. This is not to say that Protestantism was basically antinomian in the sense of being libertarian. It is to say that particularly because of Luther's doctrine of *sola fidei* there was a tendency to assume that Protestantism removed all moral shackles and restraints. Menno Simons complains about this in his *True Christian Faith*:

> They say . . . how miserably the priests have had us poor people by the nose, robbing us of the blood of the Lord, and directing us to their peddling and superstitious transactions. God be praised, we caught on that all our works avail nothing, but that the blood and death of Christ alone must cancel and pay for our sins. They strike up a Psalm, *Der Strick ist entzwei und wir sind frei*, etc. [Snapped is the cord, now we are free], while beer and wine verily run from their drunken mouths and noses. Anyone who can but recite this on his thumb, no matter how carnally he lives, is a good evangelical man and a precious brother.[4]

Again in his *Reply to False Accusations* he writes:

> All may find a place in their sect who will but keep their ceremonies, and acknowledge them to be the true preachers and

---

4. Simons, *Complete Writings*, 334.

messengers, no matter how they live, just so they keep out of the hands of the executioner. No drunkard, no avaricious or pompous person, no defiler of women, no cheat or liar, no thief, robber, or shedder of blood (I mean in the conduct of warfare), no curser or swearer so great and ungodly but he must be called a Christian. If he but say, I am sorry, then all is ascribed to his weakness and imperfection and he is admitted to the Lord's Supper, for, say they, he is saved by grace and not by merits. He remains a member of their church even though he is an impenitent and hardened godless heathen; today as yesterday and tomorrow as today, notwithstanding that the Scriptures so plainly testify that such shall not inherit the kingdom of God, for they are of the devil.[5]

Luther's concern was to get free of the multitude of things required of the faithful in Roman Christianity to achieve salvation, the prayers, penances, pilgrimages, etc. All Anabaptists joined Luther in rejecting that kind of works righteousness. But many were not so subtle; they assumed from Luther's words that works also included moral behavior, and that that too was no longer required.

Anabaptists clearly and emphatically distinguished between these ceremonial and cultic laws, and the ethical requirements of the gospel. Menno makes the difference quite clear in *True Christian Faith* when he opposes masses, holy water, pilgrimages, prayers to the saints, confessions, and fastings to "genuine, pure love and fear of God, the love and service of our neighbors" and "mercy, friendship, chastity, temperance, humility, confidence, truth, peace, and joy in the Holy Ghost."[6] The former works ought to be abandoned because they were commanded by men and because they could not deliver what was claimed for them. The latter are the expressed will of God and are the expression and fruit of eternal life.

But their insistence on doing the will of Christ was not simply a reaction to an opposite. The main point was that Jesus was Lord. He was the Master who had called them into his company. He was the one God had bidden them to obey. He exercised the authority and power of God since his resurrection. Obedience to him was obedience to God. It was a matter of their eternal destiny, of the integrity of the church, and God's plans with the world. He had called them into his purpose and they could only follow and obey. This obedience could not be a casual matter either. It was a matter of being faithful in all things, the small and the great. Hence the concern

---

5. Simons, *Complete Writings*, 569.
6. Simons, *Complete Writings*, 332–33, 342.

for what may appear to us relatively trivial matters such as the prohibition of singing.[7] The Reformed distinction between primary and secondary matters did not satisfy them because the Bible contained no criterion by which to measure what was primary and what secondary. The distinction therefore became a matter of human convenience. It should also be clearly recognized that there was a real hazard of literalism and legalism in their rejection of this distinction.

They denied that what they called the "new law" was simply another external code of behavior analogous to the law of the Old Testament. It was a law written on the heart. Jesus was for them a living Lord. They were not obeying some abstraction; he was with them in his Spirit, and it was by the power of his ever-present Spirit that they were set free to obey him. It was therefore not as their enemies said that they labored under an impossible burden. They had been set free to obey him in the doing of his will. No one forced them; they freely decided to follow. Their obedience was an expression of their inner liberation.

Again, the situation of the Anabaptist church called for strong discipline. In a world that applied all of its pressures to crush the little company one could not be casual about following Christ. As I tried to show earlier, the church was an area of order and wisdom in the midst of chaos and folly. That had to be preserved if they were to continue as disciples and as the model community. There had to be attention to detail. Hence also their practice of church discipline, even to the use of the ban and the practice of avoidance. No one who did not obey Christ according to the interpretation of the community could remain, lest the whole be infected and weakened. Herein also lay a serious hazard. The problems will be discussed below. Suffice it to say now that the reality and seriousness of the abuses accompanying the attempt to be obedient to Christ do not invalidate the attempt. It is a strange kind of logic on the part of Protestants that charges Anabaptists with legalism and lack of love when in both Roman and Protestant traditions nonconformists were dealt with great severity, imprisonment, exile with expropriation of property, and death being penalties frequently inflicted.

The fact is, however, that the Anabaptists were thoroughly biblical in their use of the term "law" or "commandment." They made a great deal of the new commandment of love in John 13:34, the fulfillment of which was

---

7. Williams and Mergal, *Spiritual and Anabaptist*, 75.

a mark of "genuine faith and true Christianity."[8] Jesus himself had called it a "new commandment" and therefore their usage rested on the highest authority. There is also frequent reference to the new law which is written not on stone tablets but on the human heart. This is based on Jer 31 and 2 Cor 3:3.[9] But the commandment to love is never merely abstract. The Zwinglian clerics, in their arguments with Anabaptists, said that everything should be governed according to faith and love, but they were weak in specifying what that meant in particular. The Anabaptists agreed with that principle but insisted further that the commandment of love is concrete and has to do with specifics in human life and experience. It means baptism of believing adults, and the Supper of fellowship limited to those who are in fact following Jesus. It means forgiveness for injury, refusal to retaliate, refusal to injure, refusal to coerce. It means aiding, supporting, and defending the needy, comforting the sorrowing, preaching the gospel to the poor. It means specifics. The commandment to love has content, usually identified as the ethical injunctions of Jesus and the apostles. And it is not a casual matter; it cannot be left to happen or not. It must be deliberately and consciously fulfilled. One must decide to do *this* rather than *that*. It is a commitment that every disciple takes upon himself at baptism, and which he regularly makes again every time he shares in the Supper.

For all their talk about law we cannot simply talk here about legalism. For no one was compelled to do these things. Those who belonged to their fellowship had with open eyes and quite deliberately entered the circle of disciples upon Jesus's own invitation. These kinds of actions flowed from within and were not imposed from without. No one who regarded their understanding of God's will as legalism was under any compulsion to join them. And if anyone already in their community could not agree he was not forced to conform against his will but was allowed to leave without restriction.

It was quite another story in Calvin's Geneva. There, because all who lived in Geneva were considered members of the church regardless of their own words and actions, specific laws governing behavior were enforced. There were fines for swearing, drinking, coming late for church, speaking disrespectfully of the preachers, failing to attend church, not being able to recite the Creed and the Lord's Prayer. People were subject to these laws and penalties whether they agreed to them or not. That is legalism. But where,

---

8. Williams and Mergal, *Spiritual and Anabaptist*, 248.
9. Williams and Mergal, *Spiritual and Anabaptist*, 79; Rideman, *Confession*, 66–67.

as in the Anabaptist fellowships, no one was baptized without the rule of Christ, that is, the commitment to accept and participate in church discipline, it is not accurate to dismiss the whole thing as legalism. Discipline, yes, but discipline is not the equivalent of legalism.

That a spirit of legalism nevertheless became evident can be accounted for on the ground that the Anabaptist way was open to it because of its attention to the details of Christian discipleship. For it is not always easy to determine whether any given act really does compromise one's position as a disciple, and this was as true then as it is today. To use an example already cited, Grebel insisted in his letter that singing is contrary to God's will. Other Anabaptists clearly did not accept this argument, otherwise we should never have had the *Ausbund*. But such issues were sometimes pressed and made the test of discipleship. It can be seen also in Menno Simons's rather rigid use of the ban of excommunication. People could not always easily decide whether a matter was important or not. There was a tendency to overestimate the seriousness of an offense. The pressure of persecution from outside surely added to the determination not to relax vigilance, and the tendency was strong to err on the side of caution.

The use of the Bible as the guide also added to the problem. This is said without disputing the necessity of using the Bible as a norm. There was, as can be seen from the example just cited, consuming concern to be faithful to God's will. The terrible array of unfaithfulness in the past drove them to the only unchanging norm there was, the Bible. It was not subject to the social, religious, or political demands of the present, and could therefore be trusted. Legalism was the farthest thing from their minds. They were simply concerned to use as faithfully as possible the one material guide they had on the straight and narrow way.

It appears that the Swiss Brethren had fallen into the trap of legalism at some points. Pilgram Marpeck wrote them a long letter on the subject of making hasty judgments and banning people for trivial reasons. They had evidently forgotten Conrad Grebel's injunction to "use determination and common prayer and decision according to faith and love, without command or compulsion."[10] It is in Marpeck's discussion that we find the most far-reaching view of Christian freedom to be found anywhere in Anabaptism. It should be said immediately that it does not appear to be representative of the whole movement. Nevertheless, it is Anabaptist and belongs to our tradition. First of all, Marpeck argues at great length that Christians

10. Williams and Mergal, *Spiritual and Anabaptist*, 79.

should not judge in haste. The image he uses is that of the flower and the fruit. Judgment ought not to be made on the basis of the leaves or blossoms but left until the fruit appears. That is to say, allowance must be made for growth in Christian discipleship. Much of what appears to be repudiation of Christ is in fact only a temporary lapse from which, with the proper love and concern on the part of his fellow disciples, a person will quickly recover. Marpeck would therefore use the ban in only extreme emergency. He appears to have been more aware than others of the potential for coercion in a closed society like an Anabaptist congregation.[11]

A special case highlights further Marpeck's understanding of Christian liberty. Evidently there were some among the Swiss who had made a rigid rule about observing the Sunday as the Old Testament Sabbath.[12] The breaker of the Sabbath, writes Marpeck, is not the one who works on a special day of the week but the one whose life is spent in efforts for himself and his own life. The Christian is not bound by any time any longer. In fact, he rules over it. In the spirit of Christ he will use it responsibly.

Scharnschlager, co-worker with Marpeck, also adds a note to this discussion in his church order. It concerns the matter of giving in the church:

> Therefore a collector of donations should be careful to receive the smallest gift as the larger one without scorn (Luke 21: 1–4), from the rich as from the poor, and faithfully thank God and the giver. Beyond that let the Lord decide. And even if someone says in carnal understanding: "After all, everyone has agreed and obligated himself to it. Why then should one not instantly demand whatever is needed?"—we reply: it will not harmonize with the order of the Holy Spirit. The work is not of man, even as it was not the flesh that agreed [to give]. Therefore it cannot be considered in a carnal, but rather in a spiritual manner. Otherwise we destroy the freedom and spontaneity of the Lord's people.[13]

Even though legally, on the basis of commitment, one could demand a donation, the person must be left free to decide what he will give, and God will pronounce the judgment. The making of hasty judgments destroys "the freedom and spontaneity of the Lord's people."

The disciple is therefore by his commitment bound to exercise love and mercy, aid and comfort to his neighbor, and to live in sincerity and

---

11. Marpeck, "Judgment and Decision," 27r–62v.
12. Marpeck, "Judgment and Decision," 46r–46v.
13. Scharnschlager, "Church Order," 134–35.

truth with all men. God in Christ has set him free from fear and hate and violence and has given him the liberty of obeying Christ, even though the cost is high. The disciple acts not from obligation but from the love of God which fills his life.

And what is it but a sense of radical freedom which enabled these people to challenge the basic religious, social, and political assumptions of their time at great cost to themselves? Men who are bound in fear and self-seeking do not act that way. They had been given some of the liberty of their Master who had walked their way before them. The next study will say more about the radicalness of the liberty they accepted.

5.5

Radical Reformation 5

Radical Politics: Anabaptism and Revolution

WALTER KLAASSEN

It may seem strange to use the word "politics" in connection with Anabaptism, since practically all the literature on the subject assumes or states that they were apolitical. It depends, of course, on what we mean by political. First of all, it should be admitted that this is to import a modern word into a historical problem. I do it in the hope that it will help to establish contact between the sixteenth and the twentieth centuries. As to the meaning of the term, the Anabaptists were apolitical, if we define the term narrowly as referring to their refusal to act as magistrates. And this is often what is meant. But if swearing the oath is a political act, then one can argue that refusing to do so is also political, since it has political consequences. It is in this broader sense that I use the word.

What gave most rulers and ecclesiastics in the sixteenth-century nightmares was what we would today call the political views of the Anabaptists; that is, their view of the nature of society, the function of the state, and its relationship to the church. The rock bottom of medieval life was the "*communitas Christiana*" or the "*corpus Christianum*," the assumption of the unquestionable unity and oneness of society, a unity in which the church and empire, pope and emperor, bishop and king, priest and nobleman share the responsibility for wholeness, peace, and order. While religiously the Reformers were clearly and undeniably innovative, socially they were all, to a man, conservative and, in the true meaning of the term, reactionary. For in some cases by default, in all with some differences, we nevertheless have largely a repetition of the medieval idea of the unity of society. While Zwingli and Luther had, to begin with, made some truly radical noises, they were soon haunted with the prospect of the secularization of the state and the dechristianization of society, and their conservatism won out.

Anabaptism came into a world in which those in authority adhered to the ideal of the *communitas Christiana*. In fact, it no longer concerned all of Christendom, but a limited area of political sovereignty. Nevertheless, the consequences for both religion and politics were largely of the same kind. The Anabaptist response to these assumptions appears to have strictly biblical origins. It is a direct consequence of their understanding of the nature of the Christian life as discipleship and their view of the church as the company of those consciously committed to Jesus. Both of these have clear biblical roots.

Conflict between Anabaptism and the prevailing assumptions on the relationships of church and civil power came at numerous points. In Zurich, in January 1525, the refusal of Conrad Grebel and some others to have their newborn infants baptized turned out to be a political act. For the city council passed a law which made baptism of infants within eight days mandatory. The establishing of a new Christian community in Zurich on January 21, 1525, was a political act *par excellence* since it was the rupturing of the unity of society. But we can perhaps best bring the matter together under four main points. These are: (1) the refusal to participate in the magistracy; (2) the refusal to take the oath; (3) the refusal to participate in violence; and (4) the insistence on religious freedom.

Refusal to Participate in the Magistracy

The refusal to participate in the magistracy is founded upon the biblical conception of the two orders, the old and the new. Menno Simons wrote of two opposing princes and two opposing kingdoms, the one characterized by peace, the other by strife.[1] Government or the magistrate functions in that kingdom where strife is the norm. Its citizens are those who do not subject themselves to God, and the magistrate was appointed to restrain

---

1. Simons, *Complete Writings*, 554.

them from evil. It is the "servant of God's anger and vengeance" and carries out its function with the sword, "to shed the blood of those who have shed blood."[2] Its function is God-given and consists of punishing the evil and defending and protecting the pious.[3] Menno Simons states it thus in addressing magistrate:

> You are called of God and ordained to your offices to punish the transgressors and protect the good, to judge rightly between a man and his fellows; to do justice to the widows and orphans, to the poor, despised stranger and pilgrim; to protect them against violence and tyranny; to rule cities and countries justly by a good policy and administration . . . to the benefit and profit of the common people.[4]

The state, then, is the restraining authority in that spiritual area which has not accepted the lordship of Christ but is subject to the prince of strife. The state exercises its restraint upon the violent with violence.

But the other area is that which has willingly and joyfully accepted the lordship. It is the domain of the prince of peace. Menno writes:

> The Prince of peace is Christ Jesus; His kingdom is the kingdom of peace, His Word is the word of peace, His body is the body of peace; His children are the seed of peace; and His inheritance and reward are the inheritance and reward of peace. In short, with this king, and in His Kingdom and reign, it is nothing but peace.[5]

The Anabaptists knew themselves to belong to this kingdom of peace. They belonged to the new order in which radically different ways of acting were the norm, and they could not participate in any actions that belonged to the old order. Therefore, also, they could not participate in the magistracy because that belonged to the old order of strife. "No Christian who makes his boast in his Lord is allowed to use and rule by violence," wrote Hans Denck. "It is not that the [magisterial] power is wrong in itself from the point of view of the evil world, for it serves the vengeance of God, but that love teaches her children a better way."[6] Menno Simons put it in this moving way: "Therefore we desire not to break this peace, but by His great

---

2. Rideman, *Confession*, 104–5.
3. Williams and Mergal, *Spiritual and Anabaptist*, 141.
4. Simons, *Complete Writings*, 551.
5. Simons, *Complete Writings*, 554.
6. Denck, *Schriften*, 85.

power by which He has called us to this peace and portion, to walk in this grace and peace, unchangeably and unwaveringly unto death."[7] If they were serious about their confession of nonviolence they could not participate in the functions of any state in their time.

But they also reversed that. By the same logic they called on the magistrate to stay out of the affairs of the new order, the church. His function essentially was a violent one and violence had no place in the church. They therefore denied the state any right to make decisions in the church or in any way to act together with the church in those things that pertain to the church. They therefore rejected the absolutist claims of the state and severely restricted its power and area of jurisdiction. It was a radical departure from an assumption practically unquestioned for more than a thousand years. The remaining three points are closely related to this basic point of view.

Refusal to Take the Oath

The basic statements on the oath found in the literature simply restate the dominical prohibition of swearing any oath at all.[8] The oath is not used by disciples of Jesus since it is designed to insure that truth is spoken. The disciple speaks the truth as a matter of course since he belongs to the truth which is Christ.

But the refusal to swear oaths brought them into direct conflict with the states of the time. For the function of the oath was not only to assure that truth was spoken; it was also employed to insure political loyalty. It had been the adhesive of feudalism and was still used in sixteenth-century Europe as a means of cementing the body politic. Thus the city of Strasburg, for example, had an institution known as the *Schwörtag* (the Day of the Oath), on which all citizens swore an oath of allegiance to the state in front of the Cathedral.[9] This oath involved fidelity as well as the readiness to support the state in time of war. Recorded incidents from 1531 and 1534 indicate that Anabaptists refused to take this oath. This, of course, cut very close to the foundation of the state. When citizens refused to swear allegiance, the state was in danger, and prosecution was the natural consequence. But Anabaptists could not in good conscience swear the oath of allegiance because it committed them to the exercise of violence and

---

7. See also Rideman, *Confession*, 108–9.
8. See Simons, *Complete Writings*, 517–21; Rideman, *Confession*, 114–20.
9. Krebs and Rott, *Elsass 1*, no. 238; Krebs and Rott, *Elsass 2*, nos. 355, 359, 374, 539.

confirmed a view of the function of the state which they could not hold. No wonder they were always suspected of sedition.

Refusal to Participate in War

It will already be clear that this refusal follows directly from the Anabaptist view of the function of the state and the disciple's relation to that. In other words, it is not an isolated position based on a Scripture passage or two. It may seem odd that they should have made so much of it when one considers that few if any of them would ever have faced actual military service. There was no conscription, for the armies were either volunteer or mercenary armies. It has been suggested, therefore, that their position on this was not particularly radical since it was largely irrelevant. But that can be asserted only by those who are either unaware of the state of affairs in Europe in the second quarter of the sixteenth century, or who do not view this part of the Anabaptist position in the religious context of the time.

It was a time of constant warfare. Charles V, emperor, was always fighting either the pope or Francis I of France. In addition, there were constant territorial wars from one end of Europe to the other. British historian J. R. Hale says:

> The one hundred years ending with 1560 were more decisive for the evolution of the art of war than any subsequent period until the late eighteenth century.... The discovery of gunpowder gradually led to a complete change [in the conduct of warfare], and since there were plenty of wars, lessons were learned quickly.... Judging from the example of the Roman Empire, men became convinced that the greatness of a nation depended in the first place upon its strength, and this in turn was supplied by a strong army. Strong military potentiality was looked upon as a guarantee for peace in which the arts and sciences could flourish, and the nation could prosper.[10]

In addition all of Europe feared the aggressiveness of the Ottoman Turks, and when Michael Sattler said he would not fight against the Turks that was something like saying that one will not fight against communism or against decadent capitalism, depending upon who the objector is. Refusal to fight meant that one was ready to let the infidels conquer Christian Europe. Even to say one would not fight, without actually refusing,

---

10. Quoted in Klaassen, et al., *No Other Foundation*, 9.

weakened the defense of Europe. Thus the Anabaptist protest against war was not made in a vacuum by any means.

Moreover, we must remember that whenever Anabaptists spoke on this matter, they were addressing themselves to professing Christians, and that the European wars were always wars between professing Christians. Anabaptists therefore were giving evidence of ecumenical concern by directing themselves against what they insisted was a glaring contradiction, Christian oral confession of allegiance to the Prince of Peace and the denial of it in action. Again Sattler's words are to the point:

> If warring were right, I would rather take the field against so-called Christians who persecute, capture, and kill pious Christians than against the Turks.... The Turk is a true Turk, knows nothing of the Christian faith, and is a Turk after the flesh. But you who would be Christians and who make your boast of Christ persecuted the pious witnesses of Christ and are Turks after the spirit![11]

I believe it quite likely that Grebel and Manz at least were influenced strongly by Zwingli's humanism at this point. Zwingli had spoken and acted strongly against the mercenary system in which the Swiss, including Zurich, had been deeply involved. Nevertheless, when we examine closely some basic statements we discover again a profound biblical orientation which at least is different in mood from the humanist brand of pacifism. It is passionate and it is uncompromising.

Grebel begins by saying that the "gospel and its adherents are not to be protected by the sword, nor are they thus to protect themselves." This is stating their basic supposition that the sword of the magistrate has nothing to do with the gospel and the church. It operates in the old order. "True Christian believers . . . do [not] use worldly swords or war, since *all* killing has ceased with them—unless, indeed, we would still be of the old law."[12] Menno Simons wrote:

> All Christians are commanded to love their enemies; to do good unto those who abuse and persecute them; to give the mantle when the cloak is taken, the other cheek when one is struck. Tell me, how can a Christian defend scripturally retaliation, rebellion, war, striking, slaying, torturing, stealing, robbing and plundering and burning cities, and conquering countries?

---

11. Williams and Mergal, *Spiritual and Anabaptist*, 141.
12. Williams and Mergal, *Spiritual and Anabaptist*, 80.

Formerly people who knew no peace, he writes, they are now called into peace.

> Therefore we desire not to break this peace, but by His great power by which He has called us to this peace ... to walk in this grace and peace, unchangeably and unwaveringly unto death.[13]

And finally Peter Rideman:

> There is therefore no need for many words, for it is clear that Christians can neither go to war nor practice vengeance. Whoever doeth this hath forsaken and denied Christ and Christ's nature.[14]

Since the Middle Ages it had been accepted practice to put dissenters and unbelievers to death. It was done for their own good, it was argued. It prevented them from falling even further into error and sometimes torture and the stake brought them to "repentance." A variant of that position showed up in Anabaptism at the infamous kingdom of God of Münster. These people argued that the only way to deal with the wicked persecuting unbelievers who would not join them was to kill them all. To these Menno writes:

> Some say, the Lord wants to punish Babylon, and that by His Christians. They must be His instruments.... All of you who would fight with the sword of David, and also be the servants of the Lord, consider these words, which show how a servant should be minded. If he is not to strive or quarrel, how then can he fight? If he is to be gentle to all men, how can he lay aside the apostolic weapons? He will need them. If he is to instruct in meekness those that oppose, how can he destroy them?[15]

Men will not come to the truth by violence and killing. Only patience and love and gentleness can accomplish that. Violence and killing are rejected in obedience to Christ because they are not the means to be used to achieve Christian ends.

---

13. Simons, *Complete Writings*, 555.
14. Rideman, *Confession*, 109.
15. Simons, *Complete Writings*, 46.

Insistence on Religious Freedom

This is of a piece with the rest of the story. Again, humanist influence is quite possible, but there is more in the Anabaptist insistence on freedom for belief than humanist idealism. The plea for this freedom for all men is simply an extension of the application of the rule of Christ. If a person within the fellowship falls, for example, uses violence upon someone and does nor repent or admit to its wrongness for a Christian, he is allowed to go his way out of the fellowship. Furthermore, it stems from Menno's description of the way in which a servant of God relates to those who do not believe. In gentleness and meekness, he is to lead them to repentance. Violence, force will not accomplish the purposes of the missionary.

Sometimes claims are made for the Protestant Reformation as the source of religious liberty. In a very broad sense this may have some validity, in that with the development of religious pluralism people had to leave one another alone. Perhaps one could say that *religious toleration* was a fruit of the Reformation. When Protestants and Catholics found that they could not militarily exterminate one another, they granted each other the toleration of exhaustion. The truth is that during the Reformation period Zwingli, Luther, and Calvin completely rejected the notion of religious liberty. Luther in 1526 said:

> Though it is not our intention to prescribe to anyone what he is to hold or believe, yet we will not tolerate any sect or division in our principality, in order to prevent harmful revolt and other mischief.[16]

Zwingli expressed himself similarly:

> Why should the Christian magistrate not destroy statues and abolish the Mass? . . . This does not mean he has to cut the priests' throats if it is possible to avoid such a cruel action. But if not, we would not hesitate to imitate even the harshest examples.[17]

And Calvin's position is well-known. He was opposed to all forms of religious toleration and insisted that one had to rid oneself of all feelings of humanity in the treatment of heretics.[18] The reasons for this intolerance are clear from their statements.

---

16. Quoted in Kamen, *Rise of Toleration*, 35.
17. Quoted in Kamen, *Rise of Toleration*, 46.
18. McNeill, *History*, 176; Kamen, *Rise of Toleration*, 79.

The simple fact of the matter is that Anabaptists, along with a few other individuals such as Sebastian Franck and Sebastian Castellio, were the first ones to raise claims for religious liberty. Balthasar Hubmaier wrote a tract called *Concerning Heretics and Those Who Burn Them* in 1524. Henry Kamen refers to this as "the earliest plea for complete toleration penned in Europe." Hubmaier says:

> One should overcome them with holy knowledge, not angrily but softly . . . If they will not be taught by strong proofs or evangelic reasons, then let them be and leave them to rage . . . The law that condemns heretics to the fire builds up both Zion in blood and Jerusalem in wickedness . . . This is the will of Christ, who said, "Let both grow together till the harvest, lest while ye gather up the tares ye root up also the wheat with them."
>
> The inquisitors are the greatest heretics of all, since, against the doctrine and example of Christ, they condemn heretics to fire, and before the time of harvest root up the wheat with the tares. For Christ did not come to butcher, destroy and burn, but that those that live might live more abundantly.[19]

Menno Simons wrote a longish plea for toleration chiefly on the basis of the proper function of the state. A good example is also Scharnschlager's appeal to the city council of Strassburg in 1534, a part of which follows:

> My dear Lords, I beg you to ask yourselves how things are with each one of you in the matter of faith. For I do not doubt that each one of you, if he love the truth, wishes to have free access to God, of his own will, indeed, to do God voluntary service, not under constraint, but uncoerced. And if you be urged to accept a faith of which you, and each one of you severally, cannot approve, you would never be able to accept such faith with a quiet conscience and would always wish to be free in the matter. Therefore I sincerely ask you, consider and take to heart that the matter stands thus with me and those with me and must so stand. Nor have we any intention to maintain ourselves and our faith with violence and military defense; but with patience and suffering to physical death in the power of God for which we pray.
>
> My dear Lords, you tell and urge us to abandon our faith and accept yours. That is as if the Emperor said to you that you should deny your faith and accept his. Now I appeal to your conscience: Do you suppose that it is right before God to obey the Emperor in this? In which case you may also say that it is right for us to obey

---

19. Kamen, *Rise of Toleration*, 60–61.

you in the similar case. But then you must also declare that you are obligated to reintroduce all the idolatry, papist monasteries, also the mass and other things. If, however, you say that it is not right before God to obey the Emperor in this, I beg and admonish you for God's sake and the sake of your soul's salvation as a poor Christian, please yield to your conscience in this, and have mercy on us poor people.[20]

He assumes that they want to be free to believe as they do; in fact, they claim that right. By their own logic they ought to extend it to others as well.

The Anabaptists themselves were denied religious liberty almost wherever they lived, and the reasons are not far to seek. Their views of the function of the state, of the oath, of violence, and religious liberty were a threat to the established order. Kamen says in his book that they represented a nuisance but no threat on account of these views. The Reformers and the hierarchy knew better. They knew long before Münster that if these ideas spread and many people adopted them, Europe would fall into chaos, that is, that the whole established order would disintegrate. Anabaptists were viewed as social revolutionaries and the identification was correct. The repeated pleas of some Mennonite historians that the Anabaptists were cruelly misunderstood are not shared by me. It is precisely because their persecutors recognized the explosive nature of what they believed and practiced that they were persecuted. This is not to say that the Anabaptists set themselves to create social revolution; that the overthrow of the established order was their avowed aim. That was true only of the Münster faction. The others were concerned to follow Jesus and to do that in the religious, social, and political sphere. But the fear of violent insurrection was the reason for resurrecting the old laws against heresy and rebaptism of Theodosius and Justinian. They were civil, not canon laws, and they were put in force again because not only the church but also the state was in danger.

The Anabaptists didn't make it; their enemies saw to that, and precisely because they were radical in their political views. No wonder the Marxists are interested in them.

---

20. Scharnschlager, "Call for Tolerance," 123.

6

The Pacifism of the Sixteenth-Century Anabaptists[21]

Harold S. Bender

A preliminary word should be said about the propriety of the use of the late, twentieth-century term "pacifism" to apply to the peace doctrines of the sixteenth-century Anabaptists. As it has been used since World War I pacifism designates broadly an idealistic antimilitaristic position whose goal is the elimination of war in history. It may be Christian or non-Christian, political or nonpolitical, but in any case, except for the radical biblical nonresistant groups such as the older Quakers and the Mennonites, it is anchored largely in a basic belief in the goodness and perfectibility of man and the reformability of the general human society on rational grounds. The original "pacifism" of the Anabaptists (and Quakers or other "historic peace churches"), as we shall see, is of a different character, with quite other roots and premises, as well as other goals. In the sixteenth century there was, in the Renaissance humanism and Erasmian pacifism, a revulsion against war and an idealistic and Christian longing for peace. But there was no peace movement as such. Erasmus, Ludovicus Vives, and Sebastian Franck were solitary figures, although it is clear that for Erasmus humanism and a certain pacifism were inseparable. Ludovicus Vives (1492–1540)

21. Reprinted from *The Mennonite Quarterly Review* 30.1 (1956).

was the most uncompromising of the humanist pacifists, but also the most pessimistic. His two pacifist works, *De Concordia et Discordia in Humana Genere* (1526, dedicated to Charles V) and *De Pacificatione* (1529, dedicated to the Archbishop of Seville), are noble statements. His basic motivation was the restoration and maintenance of Christian unity. He did not believe, however, in the possibility of world peace upon the earth; so he worked for inner peace in the individual and looked forward to real peace in eternity. Erasmus is more the humanist who is hindered in his basic work and mobility by war. Franck's *Das Kriegbüchlein des Frides* (1539) is a vigorous attack on war, as the title announces, "a war of peace battling against all alarums, revolution, and senselessness with thorough demonstration . . . that war not only does not belong in the kingdom of Christ but is nothing else than a devilish, bestial, unchristian, inhuman thing."

In the midst of the truly bloody character of the sixteenth and seventeenth centuries, both in war and religious persecution, the consistent and continued radical nonresistance of peaceful Anabaptism is remarkable with its complete rejection of war and personal violence, and its insistence upon religious liberty. About the clarity and absolutism of the Anabaptist position there can be no question, as the evidence will show in a moment. With minor exceptions such as Balthasar Hubmaier (d. 1528) and the short-lived revolutionary Münsterites (1534–1535) and Batenburgers, the entire movement from Courtrai to Königsberg and from Bern to Budapest, whether Swiss, German, Flemish, Frisian, Austrian, or Moravian, openly and vigorously broke with the universally accepted war system, or with the "sword" as they called it. For them the sword was "outside the perfection of Christ," as the Schleitheim Confession of 1527 states it.[22] Before 1525, the birth date of Anabaptism, there were, to be sure, antiwar expressions in some of the medieval nonconformist groups such as the Waldenses, and no one has exceeded Peter Chelchitzky (ca. 1460) of Bohemia in his absolutist pacifism, but by the sixteenth century the Waldenses had forgotten the antimilitarism of their fathers, and Peter's was a lone voice in the wilderness. In any case Anabaptism had no genetic connection with these prior movements; it was born in the bosom of the Reformation, and its leaders came directly out of the Roman Church or had been loyal followers of Zwingli and Luther.

Our amazement at the pacifism of the sixteenth-century Anabaptists only grows as we contemplate the belligerence of the period and the

---

22. Wenger, "Schleitheim Confession," 250.

attitudes toward war of all the leading Reformers and popes as well as the Christian princes and emperors. The Truce of God, first applied in 1076, a genuine attempt to mitigate the slaughter of feudal wars and fratricidal conflicts, had long since lost its efficacy and been discarded. *Raubrittergeist* was still abroad. The principle of an allowable just war was fixed in the dogmatic theory of the medieval Roman Church, and taken over by the Reformers (Luther at first taught only a defensive war), but where can one find any justice in the endless warrings of the sixteenth century, except possibly in the defense against the Turks? Yet all the princes were "defenders of the faith," and should have obeyed the church on this point. The wars of the century were endless. In the brief twenty-year public career of Sebastian Franck (1526–1544), the first Christian philosopher of history, who also wept over the wars of Christendom, there were four wars between France and Germany alone. Then there were the strange wars between the most Catholic Emperor Charles V, who was eager to restore the broken unity of the church, and the pope, who was the head of that church. In 1527 the troops of Charles V sacked Rome with a hitherto unheard-of slaughter, practically wiping out the cultured classes.

War was not only an accepted instrument of national or political policy. It was also an instrument of the church. Men sought to serve God by using war as an instrument of religion, of the very kingdom of God itself, as the Catholic and Protestant military leagues of the Reformation period attest. Franz von Sickingen joyfully sprang to the assistance of Luther in his ill-fated attack on the Archbishop of Treves. Admiral Coligny and his Huguenot friends took to arms to save their faith from extermination in the bloody religious wars of sixteenth-century France, as the Münsterites of 1534 had done against the Bishop of Münster's beleaguering army. And Luther called on the princes to "smite, slay, and destroy the mad dogs of peasants," whose cause he had earlier called just, for the princes would thereby be serving a good purpose. Nor should we overlook Zwingli's scheme for a great Protestant military alliance to establish the Reformation once for all against its enemies (rejected by a clearer visioned Luther), while he himself died on the battlefield of Cappel in a religious war against the Swiss Catholic cantons. It was not Thomas Müntzer alone who thought to establish God's righteousness by the sword.

Luther discussed the question of war and soldiering in the pamphlet *Ob Kreigsleute auch in seligem Stande sein können* (1526). In this pamphlet he concludes that "soldiers can be in a state of grace, for war is as necessary as eating, drinking, or any other business." But he goes even further to say, "The hand which bears the sword [i.e., the government] is as such no longer man's but God's, and not man it is, but God who hangs, breaks on the wheel, beheads, strangles."[23] Calvin abolished the distinction between the believer's private and public morality, placing the public morality of the state under the Old Testament. He held that the Sermon on the Mount cannot conflict with the politics of the pious kings of Israel and the Old Testament code.[24] Calvin defended war as a means of public vengeance against evil. Beza affirmed the rightness of religious warfare on historical, biblical, and dogmatic grounds. Troeltsch, in viewing the record of the Reformers on this question, says, "The Protestant way out of the strain of a dual morality, personal and public, is not a solution but a reformulation of the problem."[25]

In the face of such a century consider the Anabaptists. The founder of Swiss Anabaptism, Conrad Grebel, spoke clearly in his famous letter of September 1524 to Thomas Müntzer, which includes a stiff rebuke to Müntzer for his reported readiness to "use the fist" against the princes, a letter which, by the way, should go far to nullify the theory of the Münsterian origin of Anabaptism.

> True, believing Christians are as sheep in the midst of wolves. . . . They . . . must reach the fatherland of eternal rest, not by overcoming bodily enemies with the sword, but by overcoming spiritual foes. They use neither the worldly sword nor engage in war, since among them killing has ceased entirely, for we are no longer under the old covenant.[26]

Even before Grebel, in January 1523, Andreas Castelberger of the later Zurich Anabaptist circle (here I quote from the Zurich court records) was

> saying much about war; how the divine teaching is so strong against it and how it is sin. And he expressed the idea that the soldier who had plenty at home in his fatherly inheritance and goods and yet went to war, and received money and pay to kill innocent persons and to take their possessions from people who had never done him any harm, such a soldier was before Almighty God, and according to the content of Gospel teaching, a murderer and not better than one who would murder and steal on account of his

---

23. Luther, *Luther's Werke*, 626.
24. Troeltsch, *Die Soziallehren*, 637.
25. Heering, *Fall of Christianity*, 79.
26. Bender, *Conrad Grebel*, 179.

poverty, regardless of the fact that this might not be so according to human laws, and might not be counted so bad.[27]

It is important to note that both Castelberger and Grebel rejected war and killing while they were yet followers of Zwingli and before the beginning of persecution, contrary to the assertion of the chronicler Johannes Kessler, who claimed that they accepted the principle of nonresistance only after the government had enacted hostile measures against them.[28]

After the open break with Zwingli in January 1525, a steady flow of evidence is available throughout the sixteenth century in Switzerland, Germany, Holland, and Moravia on the Anabaptist testimony for Christian nonresistance and against war, killing, and the use of force in any form. Felix Manz, with Grebel a co-founder of the movement, said in December 1526, in the testimony in his trial before the Zurich court, which resulted in his martyrdom as the first Anabaptist martyr a few days later (again I quote from the court record): "It had always been his conviction and still was that no Christian could be a government officer, nor could he use the sword nor kill anyone nor punish, because he had no Scripture for it."[29] In January 1527, in a farewell letter to his brethren before his martyrdom, Manz says, "Christ never hated anyone, therefore His true servants will also not hate and will accordingly follow Christ on the road on which he has gone before us."[30]

The spokesmen of the Swiss Brethren in the Zofingen disputation of 1532 said, "In Matthew 5 Christ forbids the believers all use of force."[31] In the great Bern disputation of 1538 the Brethren spoke fully of their nonresistance, summarized as follows:

> We grant that in the non-Christian world state authorities have a legitimate place, to keep order, to punish the evil, and to protect the good. But we as Christians live according to the Gospel and our only authority and Lord is Jesus Christ. Christians consequently do not use the sword, which is worldly, but they use the Christian ban. There is a great difference between Christians and the world, the former living by the standards of the Sermon on

---

27. Bender, *Conrad Grebel*, 200.
28. Kessler, *Sabbata*, 143.
29. Muralt and Schmid, *Quellen zur Geschichte*, 216.
30. Muralt and Schmid, *Quellen zur Geschichte*, 219.
31. Bullinger, *Handlung oder Acta*, 94v.

the Mount and the latter being perverted and governed by Satan. The world uses the sword; Christians use only spiritual weapons.[32]

Without quoting other Swiss Anabaptist sources except Sattler, who will be cited later, let us accept the testimony of Bullinger, the successor to Zwingli as head of the Zurich church. In his book of 1531 against them (*Von dem unverschämpten frävel*) he quotes an Anabaptist in a fictitious dialogue as saying, "War is the worst evil that one can conceive" (*das ergist uebel das man erdenken kan*), to which the Reformed speaker in the dialogue replies, "It is truly a great evil when it is not begun and conducted with God." The Anabaptist then says further, "But do you think that the believers have even the right to go to war?" To which the Reformed speaker replies, "Yes, much and great" (*Ja vil und dick*). The Anabaptist then demands that this be proved out of God's word, which the Reformed speaker (actually Bullinger) does for almost three pages, beginning with Abraham's war against the three kings in Gen 14, and ending with John the Baptist's advice to the soldiers in Luke 3, giving examples of Christian emperors along the way, such as Constantine and Theodosius.[33] In his second book against them in 1561 (*Der Widertoufferen Ursprung*) Bullinger gives similar testimony.

> They believe that Christians should stand ready to suffer (rather than strike back). No Christian may be a ruler. The government should not undertake to regulate matters of faith and religious practice. Christians do not resist violence and do not take recourse to law. They do not use the law courts. Christians do not kill. The punishment used by them is not imprisonment and the sword, but only church discipline. They do not defend themselves, therefore they do not go to war and are not obedient to the government on this point.[34]

Appended to Bullinger's second work just mentioned is a booklet written by spokesmen of the Swiss Brethren giving their reasons why they did not make common cause with the state church. The following quotation is taken from this booklet:

> The theologians of the established church have in the first period of their reformatory labors advocated the Christian, evangelical

---

32. Staatsarchiv of Bern, "Unnütze Papiere," vol. 80.
33. Bullinger, *Der Widertöufferen*, 139v.
34. Bullinger, *Der Widertöufferen*, fol. 16.

opinion that Christians should not protect themselves or their evangelical doctrine, by worldly, carnal force, sword, weapons or resistance, nor defend themselves in this way against their adversaries and opponents, but should use only the Word of God as the Sword of the Spirit and other weapons which are mentioned in Ephesians, chapter 6; and that they should not avenge themselves, nor resist evil. The worldly, Mosaic sword should not be found among them: they should not seek justice before a court of law on account of earthly possessions or honor, but should be willing to suffer and bear the cross, if they would be Christians. And this, their former doctrine, is clearly founded on the New Testament Scriptures.[35]

Before we leave the Swiss Brethren we must report that one of the outstanding early Anabaptist leaders, Dr. Balthasar Hubmaier (martyred May 1528), did not share the nonresistant position of the Swiss Brethren. In his booklet *On the Sword*, written June 24, 1527, at Nikolsburg, Moravia, where he was the leader of a large Anabaptist congregation, he attempted to persuade the Brethren by many arguments that their antiwar position was unscriptural, and advocated the view that the Christian may use the sword both in war and as an officer of the government. The two Nikolsburg disputations of 1527, which dealt among other things with the urgent question of payment of war taxes levied by the Moravian Landtag in view of the serious threat of the Turkish advance on Vienna, resulted in a split of the congregation. Hubmaier's followers were called *Schwertler*, in contrast to the others who were called *Stäbler*. It is worthy of note that the *Schwertler* party of Hubmaier's followers soon died out (no trace is found of them after 1529), whereas the party of absolute nonresistants, who would not even pay the war tax, survived as the great Hutterite movement. The only other known Anabaptist leaders in Switzerland, Germany, or Austria-Moravia who did not share the full nonresistant position were Ambrosius Spittalmaier (martyred 1528) and Jacob Gross (recanted Anabaptism in 1531), who for a time in 1525 was a member of Hubmaier's congregation at Waldshut. While in prison at Strasbourg on August 9, 1526, Gross declared himself ready in effect for noncombatant military service. He would stand watch and carry a gun, but would not comment to take human life, "for to kill a human being is not required in any commandment of God."[36]

35. Bullinger, *Der Widertöufferen*, fol. 218v.
36. Quoted from the Strasbourg court records for 1526, see Cornelius, *Geschichte*, 268.

An outstanding case of Anabaptist nonresistant testimony is that of the noted Michael Sattler, who was ready to be nonresistant even toward the Turks. Sattler, a friend of Butzer, who called him "a dear friend of God" and "a martyr of Christ"[37] and who protested his martyrdom in May 1527, at Rottenburg on the Neckar, was probably the author of the first Anabaptist confession, the *Seven Articles of Schleitheim* of February 24, 1527, whose sixth article, "On the Sword," declares, "The sword is outside the perfection of Christ," and forbids the Christian both to bear the sword as a magistrate and to "employ it against the wicked for the defense and protection of the good, or for the sake of love."[38]

One of the most telling charges against Sattler as reported in the record of his trial,[39] published in several versions almost immediately after his execution, was the accusation that he had taught that if the Turks came into the country no resistance should be offered. Indeed, if war could be morally justified, he would rather fight against the Christians than against the Turks. This charge could not fail to make the deepest impression on the court. The Turks for years had been considered the worst foe of the empire and the Christian faith. Vast sums of money had been sacrificed by the faithful and paid as a Turkish war tax to make war on the archfoe of Christendom. King Ferdinand had been caused inexpressible distress by the Turks; at great pains he had aroused the German states and raised an army to fight them. And now the Turk was to be considered less dangerous than he and the representatives of the old faith. To be sure, Sattler was not charged, as other Anabaptists had been, with having made an alliance with the Turks, but the charge that was made was sufficient to make him an archtraitor to the empire.

Concerning this charge Sattler admitted that he had taught that if the Turk should come no armed resistance should he made, for it is written, Thou shalt not kill. We should not resist any of our persecutors with the sword, but with prayer cling to God, that he may resist and defend. Sattler even admitted having said that if war were right, he would rather march against supposed Christians who persecute, capture, and kill the God-fearing. The Turk knows nothing about the Christian faith; he is a "Turk according to the flesh." "But you want to be considered Christians, boast of

---

37. As quoted in Hulshof, *Geschiedenis*, 28.

38. Wenger, "Schleitheim Confession," 250.

39. For the bibliography of the early publication of the Sattler trial report, see Bossert, "Michael Sattler's Trial," 208.

being Christ's and still persecute His pious witnesses; you are Turks according to the spirit."⁴⁰

The infidel Turks who were before Vienna in 1529 continued to pound at the gates to the West for another century and a half. Throughout this time the Hutterite Anabaptists refused to join in the fight against them, either by taking arms, or making arms, or paying war taxes. The situation would be quite comparable to that of Western Europe today with the infidel communists threatening Western Christian civilization. Nothing could better test the sincerity and fortitude of sixteenth-century Anabaptist pacifism. Peter Rideman's classic Hutterite confession of 1515 speaks boldly:

> Now since Christ, the Prince of Peace, hath prepared and won for Himself a kingdom, that is, a Church through His own blood; in this same kingdom all worldly warfare has an end, as was promised aforetime.... Therefore a Christian neither wages war nor wields the worldly sword to practice vengeance.... Now if vengeance is God's and not ours, it ought to be left to Him and not practiced or exercised by ourselves. For, since we are Christ's disciples, we must show forth the nature of Him who though He could, indeed, have done so, repaid no evil with evil.... There is therefore no need for many words, for it is clear that Christians can neither go to war nor practice vengeance. Whosoever doeth this hath forsaken and denied Christ and Christ's nature.⁴¹

And in the time of the greatest Turkish threat (1594–1605) the Hutterites of Moravia flatly refused, under the heaviest pressure from the Emperor Rudolphus II, to pay war levies, or to grant war loans. Twice, in 1596 and 1601, the Hutterite Bishop Braidl of Neumühl, Moravia, addressed to the emperor formal letters of refusal to grant such support "for conscience' sake."⁴²

The very large and powerful Anabaptist movement in the Netherlands (until 1555 it was the strongest part of Protestantism in that corner of Europe) is well represented by its leader Menno Simons (active 1536–1561), after whom the movement was named, who repeatedly and clearly taught complete nonresistance. Three samples will suffice:

> The regenerated do not go to war, nor engage in strife. They are the children of peace who have beaten their swords into plowshares

---

40. Bossert, "Michael Sattler's Trial," 213.
41. Rideman, *Confession*, 108.
42. Zieglschmid, *Die älteste Chronik*, 575–79, 620–26.

and their spears into pruning hooks, and know of no war. They render unto Caesar the things that are Caesar's and unto God the things that are God's. Their sword is the sword of the Spirit which they wield with a good conscience through the Holy Ghost.[43]

Since we are to be conformed to the image of Christ (Rom 8:29), how can we then fight our enemies with the sword? Does not the Apostle Peter say: "For even hereunto were ye called, because Christ also suffered for us, leaving us an example, that ye should follow his steps; who did no sin, neither was guile found in his mouth; who, when he was reviled, reviled not again," etc.? (1 Pet 2:21–23; Matt 16:24).[44]

I am well aware that the tyrants who boast themselves Christians attempt to justify their horrible wars and shedding of blood, and would make a good work of it referring us to Moses, Joshua, etc. But they do not reflect that Moses and his successors, with their iron sword, have served out their time and that Jesus Christ has now given us a new commandment and has girded our loins with another sword. . . . They do not consider that they use the sword of war contrary to all evangelical Scripture against their own brethren, namely, those of like faith with them who have received the same baptism and have broken the same bread with them and are thus members of the same body.[45]

The same two thousand Anabaptist martyrs whose stories are told first in *Het Offer des Heeren* (1562 and succeeding editions) and then in the great *Martyrs' Mirror* of 1660, were without exception nonresistant. The very title of the great martyr book tells the story, *The Bloody Theatre, or Martyrs' Mirror of the Defenceless Christians Who Suffered and Were Put to Death for the Testimony of Jesus Their Saviour.*

It should be added, of course, that the Anabaptists scarcely faced the direct challenge of universal compulsory military service in the sixteenth century. The nearest to such a challenge came in Holland in 1557 when Prince William of Orange granted them exemption from military service, and the Anabaptists in turn aided the cause of Dutch independence with gifts and loans.[46]

---

43. Simons, *Complete Writings*, 170b.
44. Simons, *Complete Writings*, 435b.
45. Simons, *Complete Writings*, 198.
46. Zijpp, *Geschiedenis*, 134. See also Dyserinck, "De Weerlosheid," 104–61, 303–42; Zijpp, *De Vroegere*, 26.

The nature of the nonresistance of the sixteenth-century Anabaptists is clear from their testimonies. It is first of all biblical, and is argued from all the familiar teachings of Jesus in the Sermon on the Mount and elsewhere, as well as Rom 12, 1 Pet 2, etc., including the example of Christ and the apostles. If the examples of war in the Old Testament were brought up, the Anabaptists answered that the Old Covenant has been displaced by the New, and the teachings of Jesus supersede those of Moses and Joshua; Christ is now our Lord, not the Old Testament. Their critics were hard put to find any good answer to the scriptural argument, except to fall back upon the Old Testament and insist upon its prior and higher authority, and to add that, after all, Christ did not condemn the warriors of the Old Testament and did not specifically forbid warfare. The Anabaptists and the Reformers clearly had divergent doctrines of Scripture on the point of the relation of the two Testaments.

Calvin had no trouble at all in making the Old Testament the source of his war ethic, but for Luther, for whom personal faith in Christ was all in all, and who judged the books of the New Testament by how much they contained of Christ, it was not so simple. His solution, at least in the earlier period, was to acknowledge the law of love and nonresistance as found in the Sermon on the Mount and apply it to the personal life of the Christian, but to deny its application to the conduct of government, a solution similar in its way to the Roman Catholic ethical dualism which held the monks and the clergy to a higher stand on war than the common people. The Christian lived in two worlds, said Luther; as a citizen of the kingdom of Christ he could not fight, but as a citizen of this world he was bound to fight at the command of his prince.

Here is where the Anabaptists and Luther parted. For them there could be no such dualism. They agreed that the government had the right and necessity to use the sword, according to God's institution, but since the Christian could not use the sword, he could not take part in government. It is from this viewpoint alone that the Anabaptists declined to serve in the magistracy. They did not reject government as such; they were not anarchists.

Now one may charge the Anabaptists with being naive, but certainly they were consistent. They may not have thought through to the bitter end the logic of their withdrawal, but they at least intended to be uncompromisingly obedient to Christ and the New Testament as they understood it. Christ was for them not only a divine being to be worshiped, and a Savior from judgment, but a Master to whom they were disciples, a Lord to be followed and obeyed. They read the New Testament simply and obeyed it literally.

But how could they be so naive as to insist upon withdrawal from the government as the requirement for Christians? Was it because they were eschatologically minded and expected the near end of the world, so that it mattered little what happened to the government? There is little evidence for this, although the Hutterite chronicle speaks frequently of the times as *"diese letzte gefährliche Zeit."*

The answer is to be found rather in their doctrine of the two worlds. The new kingdom of God which is being established in their terms and through them (see Littell's discussion in his *Anabaptist View of the Church*) is of necessity distinct from the world order which is dominated by Satan. That the church and state join in persecuting the true church is only one more bit of evidence of the wickedness of the world order, they concluded. The old church (both Roman Catholic and Protestant) has failed particularly in its mixing of the two kingdoms, hence the true church must be, and is being, reestablished separate from the world. This true church is the present kingdom of Christ which is being established in the midst of and alongside of the kingdom of this world; it is not to be deferred to some millennial future.

The Anabaptists further developed a martyr-theology and a doctrine of the suffering church. The martyr church was to be able to establish its place in history through suffering. As Ethelbert Stauffer has pointed out in his valuable article in the *Zeitschrift für Kirchengeschichte* (1933) on "The Martyr-Theology of the Anabaptists," the Anabaptists saw the whole of history from the fall of the first Adam down to the Second Coming of Christ as a great battle between God and his enemies; just as Christ was victor through his cross and suffering, so the suffering church would be victorious with him in its cross and suffering, if not in the sixteenth century, at least in God's good time. For such a church nonresistance was not a weak cover for a necessary yielding to superior force; it was the supreme weapon of the Christ for conquest through his church. Here we have no idealistic or humanistic vision of getting rid of war in history; we deal rather with the very heart of Christian faith. In the evil world as it is, there is no other lot for the Christian but to suffer, but through this suffering he will conquer. So we see the Anabaptist martyrs by the hundreds going to the stake with joyful confidence, and openly turning their places of execution into evangelistic platforms. So we can understand why in some places the authorities forbade further public executions because of their attractive power in winning converts. "The blood of the martyrs," Tertullian had said long before, "is the seed of the church."

A final question concerns the relation of Anabaptist nonresistance to Erasmian pacifism. Did perhaps the early Swiss Anabaptists, or even the Dutch or the Hutterites, draw their antiwar ideas from Erasmus, who with possibly Ludovicus Vives, was the only man of outspoken pacifistic spirit in the first quarter of the sixteenth century? This question is in turn involved in the larger question of the relation of Anabaptism to humanism, particularly of the Erasmian type. The thesis of the humanistic origin of Anabaptism has been advocated by no less an authority than Walther Koehler. It has not been proved, whatever similarities there may be in the field of ethics. Anabaptism can be understood as essentially the logical unfolding of the central Reformation principles, only freed from the holdover medieval church concept of the *Corpus Christianum* with its cultural bonds. *Sola Scriptura* is sufficient to account for the pacifism of the Anabaptists. Matthew 5 persuaded Luther in his earlier years to accept personal nonresistance. It was his sense of responsibility to or solidarity with the established social order which prevented him from taking the nonresistance position to its full consequence as the Anabaptists did, just as this same concept of responsibility has kept Reinhold Niebuhr from continuing in his earlier pacifism, and no doubt keeps many other modern Christians from accepting the Christian pacifism which they believe is the authentic teaching of Jesus. Did not the Amsterdam World Council define war as mankind's greatest collective sin?

But were not some of the early Anabaptists humanists, possibly under the influence of the Erasmus who wrote *Querella Pacis* in 1516? Since Conrad Grebel himself, as well as Zwingli, under whose influence he became a Protestant, was once a humanist, I made a thorough examination of the question of the possible influence of Erasmus on Grebel in respect to the pacifist position, but without finding much light on the question.[47] In Zurich itself, in the circle of Grebel's intimate friends, there was considerable interest in the question of war and peace. As early as 1520 his good friend Oswald Myconius had written a tract against war entitled *Philirenus*, which he circulated among his friends for criticism. On August 30, 1520, Grebel had a copy in possession, which he read with great interest and "found so true" that he expressed the conviction that it deserved to be printed and

---

[47]. Bender, *Conrad Grebel*, 199–203.

thus to be made permanent. Other friends, however, were influential in persuading Myconius to withhold the pamphlet from publication. It is well known that in the years 1520–1522 and even later, the pacifist viewpoint was present in the Zwingli circle in Zurich. Zwingli had probably taken it over from Erasmus. However, the pacifist convictions of Zwingli and his friends must not have been very deep, at least not deep enough to leave any permanent influence upon their thinking, for before long Zwingli was actively engaged in planning a great military alliance to fight the pope, and as is well known he died at the head of the army of Zurich on the battlefield of Cappel in 1531. Grebel reports in a letter to Vadian in 1524, that Zwingli had preached a *kriegspredigt, et populus applausit manibus*.[48] If, then, Grebel maintained his pacifism while Zwingli lost his, there must have been some fundamental difference in the thinking of the two men on the question. This difference can probably be discovered by a comparison of the pacifism of Erasmus with the nonresistance of Conrad Grebel.

The opposition of Erasmus to war was derived primarily from a number of diverse philosophical, sociological, moral, and religious arguments, many of which are valid and useful in building up a conviction against war. But even though there is a religious tone and coloring in Erasmus's thought on the question of war and peace, as well as sincere Christian conviction, nevertheless the Erasmian pacifism was primarily humanitarian in character and not theological and biblical, except in its emphasis on the mystical unity of the body of Christ in the Sacrament. The one general argument against participation in war which Grebel used in his letter to Müntzer, the argument of "the suffering church," is not only not found in Erasmus, but is at the opposite pole from his position. A still further and significant difference between Erasmus and Grebel lies in the fact that Grebel was an absolutist on the question of war and violence, and consistently rejected all killing, including therefore wars in self-defense, whereas Erasmus, although he at times used very sharp words against war, was ready not only to permit a defensive war, but even any just war. Doctor Inez Thürlemann, who has made a thorough study of Erasmus as a pacifist, has shown in her doctoral dissertation that this was a characteristic feature of the position of Erasmus on war. She quotes him at one place as saying: "Citizens may be permitted to fight, but it must be a just war. Whether the war is just or not and in what manner and against whom it is to be fought, that must be left

---

48. Bender, *Conrad Grebel*, 274n54.

to the decision of the ruler."[49] Between the relativism of an Erasmus who would be willing to let a ruler decide whether a war was just or not, and the absolutism of a Grebel who would dare to say that "among true believing Christians killing is done away with altogether," there is considerable distance. It is probable that the humanist Conrad Grebel of 1520 to 1522 was in spirit an Erasmian pacifist, and that this opened the door of his mind to the teaching of the New Testament, particularly the Sermon on the Mount, and to the logical deduction from the fundamental concept of "the suffering church" that Christians should suffer and not fight; but the Grebel of 1525 was no longer a humanitarian pacifist but a believer in the principle of biblical nonresistance, which is something quite different.

49. Thürlemann, *Erasmus*, 44.

Anabaptism: An Introductory Bibliography

Narratives

Blanke, Fritz. *Brothers in Christ*. Scottdale: Mennonite Publishing House, 1961. A lively account of the earliest Zurich beginnings.

Dyck, Cornelius J., ed. *An Introduction to Mennonite History*. Scottdale: Herald, 1967. The first eight chapters deal with Anabaptist origins.

Other comparable treatments are:

Durnbaugh, Donald. *The Believers' Church: The History and Character of Radical Protestantism*. New York: Macmillan, 1968. Places Anabaptism within the longitudinal continuity of renewal concern from the Middle Ages to the present.

Estep, William. R. *The Anabaptist Story*. Nashville: Broadman, 1963.

Wenger, John C. *Even unto Death: The Heroic Witness of the Sixteenth-Century Anabaptists*. Richmond: John Knox, 1961.

Williams, George Huntston. *The Radical Reformation*. Philadelphia: Westminster, 1962. Places Anabaptism within the wide panorama of sixteenth-century dissidence.

Interpretation

In addition to the articles by Harold S. Bender included in this issue, the following are similar in approach:

Bender, Harold. S. "The Anabaptists and Religious Liberty in the Sixteenth Century." *The Mennonite Quarterly Review* 29.2 (1955) 83–100.

———. "'Walking in the Resurrection': The Anabaptist Doctrine of Regeneration and Discipleship." *The Mennonite Quarterly Review* 35.2 (1961) 96–110.

———. "The Zwickau Prophets, Thomas Müntzer, and the Anabaptists." *The Mennonite Quarterly Review* 27.1 (1953) 3–16.

Gish, Arthur. *The New Left and Christian Radicalism*. Grand Rapids: Eerdmans, 1970. An interpretation aimed more precisely at the social agenda of the seventies

Hershberger, Guy F., ed. *The Recovery of the Anabaptist Vision*. Scottdale: Herald, 1957. Offers interpretive material somewhat like the present issue of *Concern*, as do *The Mennonite Quarterly Review* 24.1 (1950); 35.1 (1961).

Westin, Gunnar. *The Free Church Through the Ages*. Translated by Virgil Olson. Nashville: Broadman, 1958.

Sources

Braght, Thieleman J. van. *Martyrs Mirror*. Scottdale: Herald, 1938. Continues to be reprinted in a century-old translation.

Grebel, Conrad. *Conrad Grebel's Programmatic Letters of 1524*. Transcribed and translated by John C. Wenger. Scottdale: Herald, 1970. Wenger has also produced many other brief translations in *The Mennonite Quarterly Review*.

Rideman, Peter. *Account of Our Religion, Doctrine, and Faith*. London: Hodder and Stoughton, 1950. Reprinted as *Confession of Faith*. Rifton, NY: Plough, 1970. The best available single synthetic overview of an Anabaptist.

Sattler, Michael. *The Legacy of Michael Sattler*. Translated and edited by John H. Yoder. Projected for 1971 publication (Herald) as the beginning of a new series of Radical Reformation source translations. Myron S. Augsburger's fictional *Pilgrim Aflame*. Scottdale: Herald, 1967, is based upon Sattler's life and death.

Simons, Menno. *The Complete Writings of Menno Simons*. Translated by Leonard Verduin, edited by John C. Wenger. Scottdale: Herald, 1956. The only contemporary readable translation of the complete works of a major Anabaptist writer.

Williams, George Huntston, and Angel M. Mergal, eds. *Spiritual and Anabaptist Writers: Documents Illustrative of the Radical Reformation*. Philadelphia: Westminster, 1957. Offers the only balanced collection of translated Anabaptist documents. Many such texts are translated singly and reprinted in *The Mennonite Quarterly Review* (Goshen, IN, 1927–).

Further Interest

Any major university library should provide access to *The Mennonite Quarterly Review* (Goshen, IN, 1927–) and *The Mennonite Encyclopedia* (4 vols., Herald, 1955–59). Further bibliography is provided in a flyer by Cornelius Krahn and Melvin Gingerich, eds., "The Mennonites, A Brief Guide to Information," Newton, KS: Faith and Life, 1966.

APPENDIX

Concern Republication Volumes

The original Concern pamphlet series consisted of eighteen volumes that were published between 1954 and 1971. What follows in this index is a complete listing of that content as reorganized in the seven-volume series published by Wipf and Stock.

The Roots of Concern: *Writings on Anabaptist Renewal 1952–1957*, ed. Virgil Vogt. Eugene, OR: Wipf & Stock, 2009.

Concern *for Education: Essays on Christian Higher Education, 1958–1966*, ed. Virgil Vogt. Eugene, OR: Wipf & Stock, 2010.

Concern *for the Church in the World: Essays on Christian Responsibility, 1958–1963*, ed. Laura Schmidt Roberts. Eugene, OR: Wipf & Stock, 2022.

Concern *for Church Renewal: Essays on Community and Discipleship, 1958–1966*, ed. Laura Schmidt Roberts. Eugene, OR: Wipf & Stock, 2022.

Concern *for Church Mission and Spiritual Gifts: Essays on Faith and Culture, 1958–1968*, ed. Laura Schmidt Roberts. Eugene, OR: Wipf & Stock, 2022.

Concern *for Church Polity and Discipline: Essays on Pastoral Ministry and Communal Authority, 1958–1969*, ed. Laura Schmidt Roberts. Eugene, OR: Wipf & Stock, 2022.

Appendix

Concern *for Anabaptist Renewal: A Radical Reformation Reader, 1971*, ed. Virgil Vogt and Laura Schmidt Roberts. Eugene, OR: Wipf & Stock, 2022.

***The Roots of* Concern: *Writings on Anabaptist Renewal 1952–1957*,** ed. Virgil Vogt. Eugene, OR: Wipf & Stock, 2009.

Virgil Vogt, "Foreword"

Paul Peachey, "The Historical Genesis of the Concern Project"

The Original Frontispiece of Concern Volumes 1–4

Concern 1 (1954)
    Paul Peachey, "Introduction"
    Paul Peachey, "Toward an Understanding of the Decline of the West"
    John Howard Yoder, "The Anabaptist Dissent: The Logic of the Place of the Disciple in Society"

Concern 2 (1955)
    Paul Peachey, "Preface"
    John W. Miller, "The Church in the Old Testament"
    Paul Peachey, "Spirit and Form in the Church of Christ"
    David A. Shank and John Howard Yoder, "Biblicism and the Church"
    Appendix: "Close Communion—On What Lines?"

Concern 3 (1956)
    Paul Peachey, "Preface"
    C. Norman Kraus and John W. Miller, "Intimations of Another Way: A Progress Report"
    Hans-Joachim Wiehler, "Preaching in the Church?"
    J. Lester Brubaker and Sol Yoder, "A Concern Retreat [Concern and Camp Luz]"
    Lewis Benson, "The Call: Journal of Spiritual Reformation"
    Notes on books

Concern 4 (June 1957)
    Paul Peachey, "Preface"
    "Epistolary: An Exchange by Letter"
    Paul Peachey, "What Is Concern?"

John Howard Yoder, "What Are Our Concerns?"

John W. Miller, "Organization and Church"

Herbert Klassen, "Property: A Problem in Christian Ethics"

CONCERN *for Education: Essays on Christian Higher Education, 1958–1966*, ed. Virgil Vogt. Eugene, OR: Wipf & Stock, 2010.

Virgil Vogt, "Editor's Note"

Michael Cartwright, "Foreword"

John Howard Yoder, "Christian Education: Doctrinal Orientation" (1959)

John Howard Yoder, "A Syllabus of Issues Facing the Church College" (1964)

John Howard Yoder and Paul M. Lederach, "Theological Statements for a Philosophy of Mennonite Education" (1971)

CONCERN 13 (1966)

Albert J. Meyer and Walter Klaassen, "Church and Mennonite Colleges"

Joanne Zerger Janzen, "The Bethel Experience in Retrospect"

Walter Klaassen, "Christian Life at Conrad Grebel College"

Henry Rempel, "The Bluffton College Christian Fellowship"

Steve Behrends, "Christian Communal Living on the Tabor Campus"

[Unattributed] "Tabor Christian Fellowship Association"

Glenn M. Lehman, "The Church on Eastern Mennonite College Campus"

Harold E. Bauman, "The Church on Campus, Present and Future: What Are the Issues?"

Virgil Vogt, "Afterword"

CONCERN *for the Church in the World: Essays on Christian Responsibility, 1958–1963*, ed. Laura Schmidt Roberts. Eugene, OR: Wipf & Stock, 2022.

Laura Schmidt Roberts, "Series Foreword"

Laura Schmidt Roberts, "Introduction"

Gordon D. Kaufman, "Nonresistance and Responsibility" (CONCERN 6, 1958)

APPENDIX

Albert J. Meyer, "A Second Look at Responsibility" (CONCERN 6)

David Habegger, "Nonresistance and Responsibility—A Critical Analysis" (CONCERN 7, 1959)

John Howard Yoder, "The Otherness of the Church" (CONCERN 8, 1960)

CONCERN 10 (1961)

Jan M. Lochmann, "Christian Thought in the Age of the Cold War"
Albert Gaillard, "Christians and Marxists"
Katharina van Drimmelen, "Where Are the Firemen?"
John Howard Yoder, "The Christian Answer to Communism"
John Howard Yoder, "Marginalia"

CONCERN 11 (1963)

Karl Barth, "Poverty"
Andrew Murray, "The Poverty of Christ"
R. Mehl, "Money"
Virgil Vogt, "God or Mammon"
John Howard Yoder, "Marginalia"

Melissa Florer-Bixler, "All Economy Is Atheist: Towards a Non-Competitive Hope for the Church in the World"

Appendix: CONCERN republication volumes content list

CONCERN *for Church Renewal: Essays on Community and Discipleship, 1958–1966*, ed. Laura Schmidt Roberts. Eugene, OR: Wipf & Stock, 2022.

Laura Schmidt Roberts, "Series Foreword"

Laura Schmidt Roberts, "Introduction"

John Howard Yoder, "Marginalia" excerpt (CONCERN 8, 1960)

John Howard Yoder, "Marginalia" excerpt (CONCERN 5, 1958)

Hans-Ruedi Weber, "The Church in the House" (CONCERN 5)

Quintus Leatherman, "The House Church in the New Testament" (CONCERN 5)

Paul M. Miller, "Can the Sunday School Class Be the 'House' within which the True Church Is Experienced?" (CONCERN 5)

Albert Steiner, "Group Dynamics in Evangelism [by Paul Miller]: A Review Article" (Concern 8)

Gerald C. Studer, "Evangelism Through the Dynamics of a Christian Group" (Concern 5)

Virgil Vogt, "Small Congregations" (Concern 5)

Concern 12 (1966)
   Leland Harder, "Changing Forms of the Church and Her Witness"
   John W. Miller, "The Renewal of the Church"
   John Howard Yoder, "Marginalia: A Syllabus of Issues"

Lewis Benson, "The Order that Belongs to the Gospel" (Concern 7, 1959)

Susanne Guenther Loewen, "After Yoder: Failure, Authenticity, and the Renewal of the Mennonite Church"

César García, "A Global Communion as a Condition for the Possibility of Church Renewal"

Appendix: Concern republication volumes content list

Concern *for Church Mission and Spiritual Gifts: Essays on Faith and Culture, 1958–1968*, ed. Laura Schmidt Roberts. Eugene, OR: Wipf & Stock, 2022.

Laura Schmidt Roberts, "Series Foreword"

Laura Schmidt Roberts, "Introduction"

Paul Peachey, "Churchless Christianity" (Concern 7, 1959)

M. H. Grumm, "The Search for Guaranteed Survival" (Concern 8, 1960)

Edmund Perry, "The Christian Mission to the Resurgent Religions" (Concern 9, 1961)

John Howard Yoder, "A Light to the Nations" (Concern 9)

Paul Peachey, "The End of Christendom" (Concern 9)

Concern 15 (1967)
   John Howard Yoder, "Marginalia"
   James Fairfield, "Tongues, a Testimony"
   Herb Klassen and Maureen Klassen, "You Shall Receive . . ."

APPENDIX

S. Djojodihardijo, "An Experience in My Life"

Donald R. Jacobs, "The Charismatic in East Africa"

Myron S. Augsburger, "The Charismatic Aspects of the Work of the Spirit"

Irvin B. Horst, "A Historical Estimate of the Charismatic Movement"

Gerald C. Studer, "The Charismatic Revival: A Survey of the Literature"

Werner Schmauch, "The Prophetic Office in the Church" (CONCERN 5, 1958)

CONCERN 16 (1968)

Henderson Nylrod, "Nasty Noel"

William Roberts Miller, "Pious Jingle Bells and the Coming of Christ"

Marlin Jeschke, "Getting Christ Back Out of Christmas"

John Howard Yoder, "On the Meaning of Christmas"

John Howard Yoder and Virgil Vogt, "Marginalia: The Case Against Christmas"

Hyung Jin Kim Sun, "Global Anabaptist Movement: From Cross-cultural to Multicultural to Intercultural"

Andrés Pacheco Lozano, "Mission and Margin(alization): An Ecumenically-Shaped Anabaptist/Mennonite Approach to Mission"

Appendix: CONCERN republication volumes content list

CONCERN *for Church Polity and Discipline: Essays on Pastoral Ministry and Communal Authority, 1958–1969*, ed. Laura Schmidt Roberts. Eugene, OR: Wipf & Stock, 2022.

Laura Schmidt Roberts, "Series Foreword"

Laura Schmidt Roberts, "Introduction"

Gerald C. Studer, "Second Thoughts on the Pastoral Ministry" (CONCERN 6, 1958)

[Unattributed] "Marginalia" excerpt (CONCERN 6)

A. H. A. Bakker, "Efficiency in the Church" (CONCERN 7, 1959)

Edgar Metzler, "The Need to Which We Minister" (CONCERN 7)

Lewis Benson, "The Church's One Foundation" (CONCERN 8, 1960)

Walter Klaassen, "The Preacher and Preaching" (CONCERN 9, 1961)

William Klassen, "Discipleship and Church Order: A Review and Discussion" (CONCERN 9)

Walter Klaassen, "New Presbyter is Old Priest Write Large" (CONCERN 17, 1969)

J. Lawrence Burkholder, "Theological Education for the Believers' Church" (CONCERN 17)

Virgil Vogt, "Marginalia" excerpt (CONCERN 17)

Elmer Ediger, "*Studies in Church Discipline*: A Review Article" (CONCERN 5, 1958)

William Klassen, "Some Neglected Aspects in the Biblical View of the Church" (CONCERN 8)

Calvin Redekop, "Postulates Concerning Religious Intentional Ethnic Groups" (CONCERN 9)

Balthasar Hubmaier, "On Fraternal Admonition" (CONCERN 14, 1967)

Don Jacobs, "Walking Together in East Africa" (CONCERN 14)

Samuel Shoemaker, "Dealing with Other People's Sins" (CONCERN 14)

Kimberly Penner, "Toward Ecclesial Practices and Notions of Authority that Embody Radical Hope"

Isaac S. Villegas, "The Ecclesial Flesh of Anabaptist Visions"

Appendix: CONCERN republication volumes content list

CONCERN *for Anabaptist Renewal: A Radical Reformation Reader, 1971*, ed. Virgil Vogt and Laura Schmidt Roberts. Eugene, OR: Wipf & Stock, 2022.

Editor's Note

John Roth, "Foreword"

CONCERN 18 (1971)

   Virgil Vogt, "Introduction"

   John Howard Yoder, "The Recovery of the Anabaptist Vision"

   Harold S. Bender, "The Mennonite Conception of the Church and Its Relation to Community Building"

   Harold S. Bender, "The Anabaptist Theology of Discipleship"

   William Klassen, "Anabaptist Studies"

Appendix

Walter Klaassen, "Radical Reformation"
Harold S. Bender, "The Pacifism of the Sixteenth Century Anabaptists"
"Anabaptism: An Introductory Bibliography"

Appendix: Concern republication volumes content list

Bibliography

Anabaptist Mennonite Biblical Seminary. "AMBS Response to Victims of John H. Yoder Abuse." https://www.ambs.edu/about/ambs-response-to-victims-of-yoder-abuse.
Bender, Harold S. *Conrad Grebel*. Goshen: Mennonite Historical Society, 1950.
———. "Conrad Grebel." In *The Mennonite Encyclopedia*, 2:566–75. Scottdale: Mennonite Publishing House, 1959.
———. "Pilgram Marpeck: Anabaptist Theologian and Engineer." *The Mennonite Quarterly Review* 38.3 (July 1964) 231–65.
Blanke, Fritz. *Brothers in Christ*. Scottdale: Mennonite Publishing House, 1961.
Bonhoeffer, Dietrich. *The Cost of Discipleship*. London: SCM, 1959.
Bossert, Gustav, Jr. "Michael Sattler's Trial and Martyrdom in 1527." *The Mennonite Quarterly Review* 25.3 (July 1951) 201–18.
Bullinger, Heinrich. *Der Widertöufferen Ursprung, Fürgang, Secten, Wäsen*, Zurich: Froschauer, 1561.
———. *Handlung oder Acta gehaltener Disputation und Gespräch zu Zoffingen inn Berner Biet mit den Widertöufferen*. Zurich: Froshauer, 1532.
Clasen, Claus-Peter. "The Sociology of Swabian Anabaptism." *Church History* 32.2 (1963) 150–80.
Cornelius, Carl A. *Geschichte des Münsterischen Aufruhrs*. Vol. 2. Leipzig: Weigel, 1860.
Cramer, David, et al. "Theology and Misconduct: The Case of John Howard Yoder." *The Christian Century*, August 20, 2014. https://www.christiancentury.org/article/2014-07/theology-and-misconduct.
Denck, Hans. *Hans Denck: Schriften II*. Edited by Walter Fellman. Gütersloh: Bertelsmann, 1956.
Dyck, Cornelius J. "From Ignatius to Wyclif." *Mennonite Life* 19.2 (1964) 79–83.
———, ed. *An Introduction to Mennonite History*. Scottdale: Herald, 1967.
Dyserinck, Joh. "De Weerlosheid volgens de Doopsgezinden." *De Gids* 54 (1890) 104–61, 303–42.
Estep, William R. *The Anabaptist Story*. Nashville: Broadman, 1963.
Fosdick, Harry E. "The Schleitheim Confession of Faith." In *Great Voices of the Reformation*, 286–95. New York: Random House, 1952.
Franck, Sebastian. *Chronica, Zeitbuch und Geschichtsbibel*. Strasbourg: Balthasar Beck, 1531.

Bibliography

Heering, Gerrit J. *The Fall of Christianity*. Translated by J. W. Thompson. London: Allen and Unwin, 1930.

Hubmaier, Balthasar. *Balthasar Hubmaier: Schriften*. Edited by Westin von Gunnar and Torsten Bergsten. Gütersloh: Gerd Mohn, 1962.

Hulshof, Abraham. *Geschiedenis van Doopsgezinden te Straatsburg van 1525 tot 1557*. Amsterdam: J. Clausen, 1905.

Hut, Hans. "The Mystery of Baptism." In *Der Linke Flügel der Reformation*, edited by Heinhold Fast, 79–99. Bremen: Carl Schünemann, 1962.

———. "Of the Mystery of Baptism." *Patterns of Reformation*, translated by George Rupp, 379–99. London: Epworth, 1969.

Kamen, Henry. *The Rise of Toleration*. New York: World University Library, 1967.

Kessler, Johannes. *Johannes Kesslers Sabbata, mit kleineren Schriften und Briefen*. St. Gall, 1902.

Kiwiet, Jan J. "The Life Hans Denck." *The Mennonite Quarterly Review* 31.4 (1957) 227–59.

———. *Pilgram Marbeck*. Kassel: J. G. Oncken, 1957.

———. "The Theology of Hans Denck." *The Mennonite Quarterly Review* 32.1 (1958) 3–27.

Klaassen, Walter. "The Bern Debate of 1538: Christ the Center of Scripture." *The Mennonite Quarterly Review* 40.2 (1966) 148–56.

Klaassen, Walter, et al. *No Other Foundation: Commemorative Essays on Menno Simons*. Newton, KS: Bethel College, 1962.

Klassen, Herbert. "Ambrosius Spittlemaier." In *The Mennonite Encyclopedia* 4:559–601.

———. "The Life and Teaching of Hans Hut." *The Mennonite Quarterly Review* 33.3 (1959) 171–205; 33.4 (1959) 267–304.

Klassen, William. *Covenant and Community: The Life, Writings, and Hermeneutics of Pilgram Marpeck*. Grand Rapids: Eerdmans, 1968.

———. *The Forgiving Community*. Philadelphia: Westminster, 1966.

Krebs, Manfred, and Hans Georg Rott, eds. *Elsass 1. Teil Stadt Strassburg 1522–1532*. Quellen zur Geschichte der Täufer 7. Gütersloh: Gerd Mohn, 1959.

———. *Elsass 2. Teil Stadt Strassburg 1533–1535*. Quellen zur Geschichte der Täufer 8. Gütersloh: Gütersloher Verlag-Haus, 1960.

Luther, Martin. *D. Martin Luthers Werke* (Weimarer Ausgabe). Vol. 19. Weimar: Hermann Böhlaus, 1887.

Marpeck, Pilgram. "Judgment and Decision." In *Das Kunstbuch*, edited by Jörg Propbst Rothenfelder gen. Maler, 27v–62r. Burgerbibliothek Bern, Cod. 464, 1561.

———. "Pilgram Marpeck's Confession of Faith Composed at Strasburg, December 1531–January 1532." Transcribed and edited by John C. Wenger. *The Mennonite Quarterly Review* 12.3 (1932) 167–202.

McNeill, John T. *The History and Character of Calvinism*. New York: Oxford University Press, 1967.

Muralt, Leonhard von. *Glaube und Lehre der schweizerischen Wiedertäufer in der Reformationszeit*. Zurich: Beer, 1938.

Muralt, Leonhard von, and Walter Schmid. *Quellen zur Geschichte der Täufer in der Schweiz*, Erster Band. Zurich: Theologischer Verlag, 1952.

Ridemann, Peter. *Confession of Faith: Account of Our Religion, Doctrine and Faith*. London: Hodder and Stoughton, 1950.

Roberts, Laura Schmidt. *Concern for Church Mission and Spiritual Gifts: Essays on Faith and Culture, 1958–1968*. Eugene, OR: Wipf & Stock, 2022.

Bibliography

———. *Concern for Church Polity and Discipline: Essays on Pastoral Ministry and Communal Authority, 1958–1969*. Eugene, OR: Wipf & Stock, 2022.

———. *Concern for Church Renewal: Essays on Community and Discipleship, 1958–1966*. Eugene, OR: Wipf & Stock, 2022.

———. *Concern for the Church in the World: Essays on Christian Responsibility, 1958–1963*. Eugene, OR: Wipf & Stock, 2022.

Scharnschlager, Leupolt. "A Call for Tolerance." In *Der Linke Flügel der Reformation*, edited by Heinhold Fast, 119–30. Bremen: Carl Schünemann, 1962.

———. "A Church Order for Members of Christ's Body." In *Der Linke Flügel der Reformation*, edited by Heinhold Fast, 130–37. Bremen: Carl Schünemann, 1962.

Simons, Menno. *The Complete Writings of Menno Simons*. Translated by Leonard Verduin. Edited by John C. Wenger. Scottdale: Herald, 1956.

Soto Albrecht, Elizabeth, and Darryl W. Stephens, eds. *Liberating the Politics of Jesus: Renewing Peace Theology through the Wisdom of Women*. London: T. & T. Clark, 2020.

Staatsarchiv of Bern. "Unnütze Papiere." In *Acta des Gesprächs zwüschenn predicannten und Touffbrüderenn*, 1538 (unpublished manuscript of Bern disputation). Vol. 80.

Thürlemann, Inez. *Erasmus von Rotterdam und Joannes Ludovicus Vives als Pazifisten*. Freiburg, Switzerland: St. Paulusdruckerei, 1932.

Tillich, Paul. *A Complete History of Christian Thought*. New York: Harper & Row, 1968.

Troeltsch, Ernst. *Die Soziallehren der christlichen Kirchen und Gruppen*. Tübingen: Mohr, 1912.

Vogt, Virgil. *CONCERN for Education: Essays on Christian Higher Education, 1958–1966*. Eugene, OR: Wipf & Stock, 2010.

———. *The Roots of CONCERN: Writings on Anabaptist Renewal 1952–1957*. Eugene, OR: Wipf & Stock, 2009.

Waltner Goossen, Rachel. "'Defanging the Beast': Mennonite Responses to John Howard Yoder's Sexual Abuse." *Mennonite Quarterly Review* 89.1 (2015) 7–80.

Wenger, John C. "The Schleitheim Confession." *The Mennonite Quarterly Review* 19.4 (1945) 243–53.

Williams, George Huntston. *The Radical Reformation*, 118–48, 435–76. Philadelphia: Westminster, 1962.

Williams, George Huntston, and Angel M. Mergal, eds. *Spiritual and Anabaptist Writers: Documents Illustrative of the Radical Reformation*. Philadelphia: Westminster, 1957.

Yoder, John Howard. *Die Gespräche zwischen Täufern und Reformatoren in der Schweiz, 1523–1538*, 1–79. Karlsruhe: Schneider, 1962.

Zieglschmid, Andreas J. F., ed. *Die älteste Chronik der Hutterischen Brüder*. New York: Carl Schurz Memorial Foundation, 1943.

Zijpp, Nanne van der. *De Vroegere Doopsgezinden en de Krijgsdienst*. Wolvega: Taconis, 1930.

———. *Geschiedenis der Doopsgezinden in Nederland*. Arnhem: Van Loghum Slaterus, 1952.

www.ingramcontent.com/pod-product-compliance
Lightning Source LLC
Chambersburg PA
CBHW071232170426
43191CB00032B/1352